GOOGLE ADWORDS

The Practical Guide for Small Businesses

MORE traffic

MORE customers

MORE sales

BIGGER profits for your business

By Jackie Key

www.jackie-key.com

Google AdWords: The Practical Guide for Small Businesses

Author: Jackie Key
Cover Design: Tony Johnson www.tonyjohnsoncreativedesign.co.uk
Production and Composition: Sarah Houldcroft www.VAforAuthors.com

© Copyright 2015 Jackie Key
All rights reserved.

No part of this book may be reproduced in any form without permission in writing from the author. Reviewers may quote brief passages in reviews. Thank you for respecting my work. No part in this publication may be reproduced or transmitted in any form or by any means, mechanical or electronic, including photocopying or recording, or by any information storage and retrieval system, or transmitted by email without permission in writing from the publisher.

While all attempts have been made to verify the information provided in this publication, neither the author nor the publisher assumes any responsibility for errors, omissions, or contrary interpretations of the subject matter herein.

Adherence to all applicable laws and regulations, including international, federal, state and local governing professional licensing, business practices, advertising, and all other aspects of doing business in the U.K., U.S., Canada or any other jurisdiction is the sole responsibility of the purchaser or reader. The reader is responsible for his or her own actions.

Neither the author nor the publisher assume any responsibility or liability whatsoever on behalf of the purchaser or reader of these materials. The author does not accept any responsibility for any loss, which may arise as a consequence of reliance on information contained in this book.

Registered trademarks acknowledged. Google AdWords is a trademark of Google Inc.

The information in this book and in particular the screenshots provided from the Google AdWords system are correct at the time. Google continue to change their system and so some may be out-of-date or will have changed.

Any perceived slight of any individual or organization is purely unintentional.

ISBN: 978-1512082715

Dedicated to my gorgeous partner Emma, my wonderful daughter Lucy, and Rosie our faithful Labrador who have all supported me throughout the writing of this book. I love all of you with all my heart.

'This book is a must read for everyone looking to use Google AdWords. Easy to read and really practical with some great tips. Simply excellent content. After reading the book I've been able to develop my first AdWords campaign and I've got results from day one!'

Nick Pratt, Web Traffic Lounge

'Great book. Clear, concise and easy to read but most importantly really useful. I refer back to it again and again.'

Paul Chapman, Secret Marketing Coach

'Well done on this book, Jackie, really interesting and informative. It was easy to read, easy to navigate and easy to understand.'

B. Mackenzie, Marketing Manager, TMS Motor Group Limited

Contents

Abbreviations 1

Foreword 2

Chapter One - An Introduction To Google Adwords 3

    In the Beginning 3

    Where Your Advert Would Appear 4

    What Google Wants 6

    What You Want 6

    Making Google Adwords Work for You 7

    Go On, Take The Plunge… 8

    Rapid Recap 8

Chapter Two - Your business – Are you ready? 9

    Defining Both Yourself and Your Customer 9

    Are You Ready? 11

    Understanding the Lifetime Value of Your Customer 12

    Rapid Recap 14

Chapter Three - Keyword Research 15

    Identifying Your Customers Before Your Keywords 16

    Finding Your Keywords 17

    Using Google's Keyword Planner 20

    Grouping Your Keywords 24

    Different Types of Keywords 25

    Rapid Recap 28

    Chapter Checklist 29

Chapter Four - Adwords Campaign Set Up 30
- The Structure of Adwords 30
- Creating an Account 31
- Setting Up More Campaigns 39
- Creating Your Ad Group and Ad 47
- Adding Your Negatives 50
- Eat, sleep, **SPLIT TEST**, REPEAT 51
- Rapid Recap 53
- Chapter Checklist 54

Chapter Five - Improving your Ad 55
- Writing the Killer Advert 55
- The Advert Breakdown 55
- Every Word Counts: Power Words and Calls to Action 58
- Ad Extensions 59
- Rapid Recap: 64

Chapter Six - Landing Pages that Convert 65
- The Three Golden Rules 65
- Improving Your Landing Pages 68
- Rapid Recap 70

Chapter Seven - Conversion Tracking 72
- What is Conversion Tracking? 72
- Step by Step Way To Set Up Conversion Tracking Through Google Adwords 73
- Google Analytics and Tracking 81
- Adding Conversion Columns at All Levels 82
- Rapid Recap 83
- Chapter Checklist 83

Chapter Eight - Quality Score 85

How to Access Your Quality Score 85

Why Quality Score is Crucial! 90

Understanding Your Quality Score 87

What Does Your Quality Score Assess? 88

Improving Your Adwords Campaigns to Improve Your Quality Score 89

Chapter Nine - Campaign Optimisation 92

Why Campaign Optimisation? 92

Search Terms All Report and Its Use 92

The Peel and Stick Process 95

Removing Zero Impression Keywords 99

Optimising Bids 99

Advert Improvements 101

Landing Pages 102

Rapid Recap 102

Chapter Checklist 103

Chapter Ten - Other Google Networks 105

What is the Google Display Network? 105

How Does It Work? 105

Search VS Display - Which Does What? 106

How to Choose Who to Target 107

Setting Your Bidding Options 108

How to Succeed at Interruption Marketing 108

Remarketing on GDN 109

Rapid Recap 111

Here's to your success with Google Adwords! 112

Appendix - Power Words 116

Appendix - Negative Words To Consider 117

Glossary 118

References 123

About The Author 124

Acknowledgements 125

Index 126

ABBREVIATIONS

CPA   Cost Per Action or Cost Per Acquisition

CPC   Cost Per Click

CPM   Cost Per Thousand

CTR   Click Through Rate

GCO   Google Conversion Optimiser

GDN   Google Display Network

PPC   Pay Per Click

ROI   Return On Investment

SEO   Search Engine Optimisation

FOREWORD
A LITTLE NOTE TO YOU MY READER

This book can help you to build your business fast – using the power of Google AdWords.

In today's world, whether we like it or not, you can do pretty much anything online; socialising, shopping, banking... the list goes on, and of course Marketing is not exempt from this. As a small business owner it is easy to assume that this fast paced, highly competitive world just isn't for you, but in thinking this, you couldn't be more wrong. In fact one of the key principles behind Google AdWords is that spending power isn't the be all and end all. The truth is small businesses have an equal chance at succeeding as multinational corporations. Using complicated algorithms, Google has devised a way to level the playing field so that those with big purses cannot simply pay their way to the top. And whilst AdWords has been around for many years, you haven't missed the boat.

This book is filled with easy to follow step by step processes and handy tips and checklists to help you, the small business owner, conquer AdWords without having to delve too deeply into your pockets, or even having to hire someone to manage it for you.

AdWords can be used by anyone, all you have to do is learn the rules, play the game and watch as your winnings come in.

Read this book, implement and then for more tips, tricks and video tutorials check out the online Google AdWords Academy at www.jackie-key.com containing over 20 videos. If you want to buy the course, as a thank you for purchasing this book, simply add MANUAL at the checkout and you'll get 25% off the usual Google AdWords Academy price.

CHAPTER ONE
AN INTRODUCTION TO GOOGLE ADWORDS

<u>In the Beginning</u>

The importance of the internet in today's world cannot be overstated, nor can the supremacy of the superpower that is Google. Our everyday lives revolve around the use of the internet, and in particular Google. Daily problems and queries can often be solved by one simple instruction; 'Google it'.

How old is Bill Gates? (We Google people's age all the time apparently…) How do you make scrambled eggs? 'Google it.' (Obviously, knowing how to get the balance between being too rubbery and too watery is absolutely essential!) When do babies start teething? 'Google it'. I keyed this into Google and guess what; there was a Google ad at the top by Calpol!

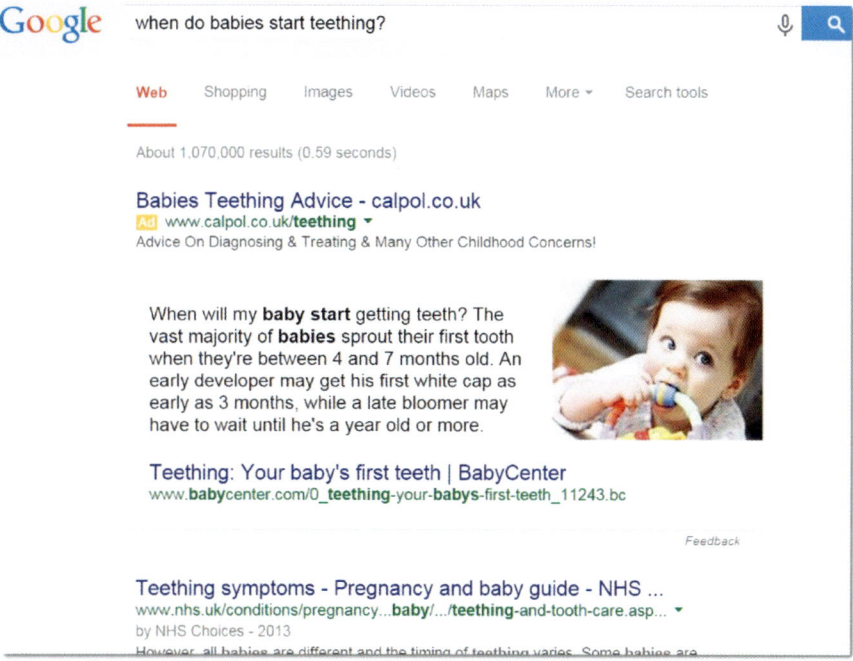

The fact that Google has managed to turn itself from simply being a noun into a commonly used verb proves beyond all shadow of a doubt, that it has reached number one.

Over the last few decades, Google has beaten its competition. Once significant search engines like Hotbot, Altavista, Excite and Infoseek have fallen into the shadows of the mighty Google, which now reigns supreme over the worldwide web. Every second 70,000 searches are typed into Google, which is 60 billion per day.[1]

Of course the internet now has a vital role to play in the marketing of businesses. However the first site which provided opportunities for companies to advertise online was not the brainchild of Google, but in fact a company called Idealab, who created GoTo.com. At the time of its release, GoTo.com was unique in the opportunities it offered its business customers; there was a direct link between the goals of buyers and sellers, advertisers paid per impression (appearance on a search results page), and most importantly anyone could join, hassle free and cost free.

Yet the days of GoTo.com were numbered. It wasn't long before Google caught on to the idea, and in 2000 it created Google AdWords. In 2002 made the 'game changer' move which would confirm them as number one. Rather than charging per impression they charged per click - a much more attractive deal for those who wanted to advertise on the internet. Having started with only 350 customers, Google AdWords has gone from strength to strength. In 2011 Google "generated $37.9 billion, largely due to advertising"[2]...and it keeps on growing.

The great thing about this incredible resource is that it is right at your fingertips. You don't have to download some complicated programme; you don't have to pay through the nose, order it or even pay up front... Simply go onto Google, create your AdWords account and get started!

Where Your Advert Would Appear
Even though Google has been allowing organisations to advertise on Google since 2000, not everyone is aware of the difference between the adverts and the 'natural' or 'organic' listings. Basically, the AdWords adverts appear at the very top of a search results page and down the right hand side of the page, highlighted in an orange box or by a small orange 'Ad' symbol next to it.

Here is a results page for 'florist Nottingham' with the adverts and organic results highlighted.

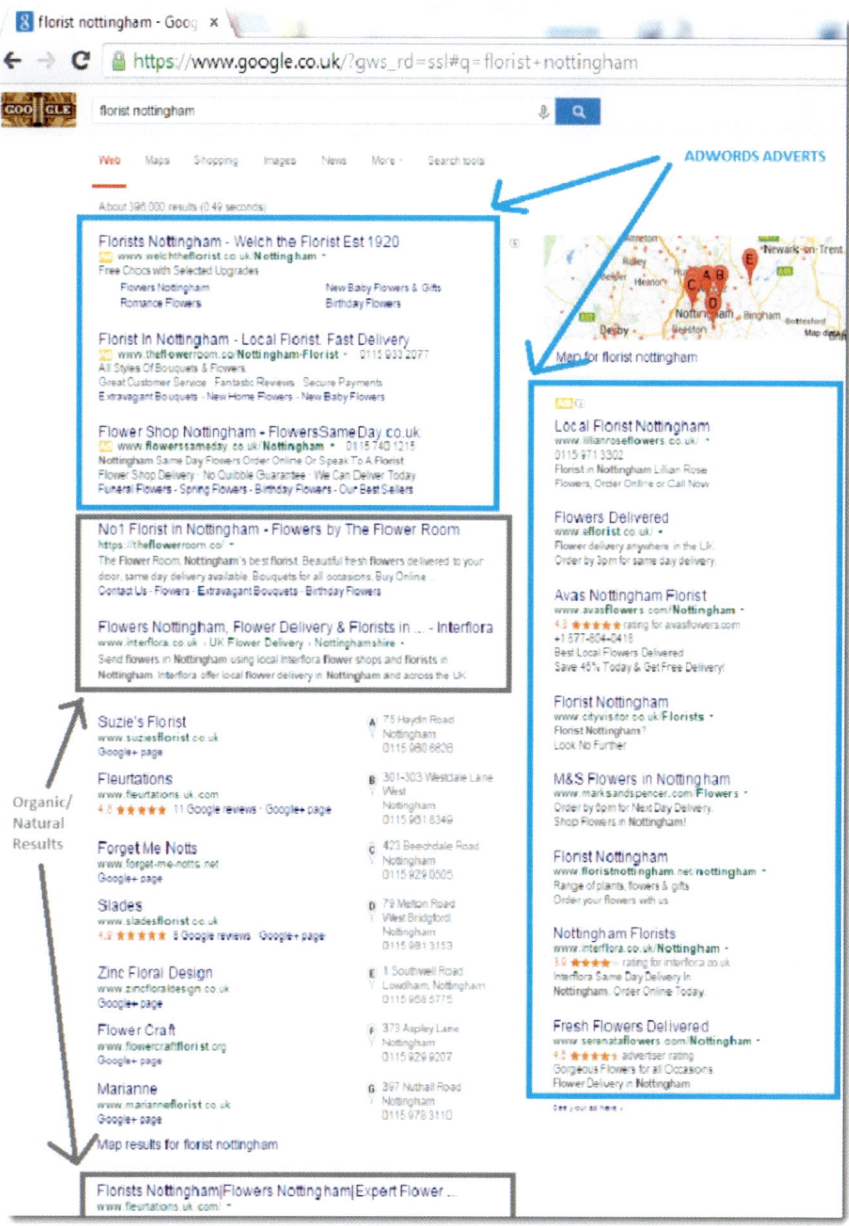

So your advert would appear at the top or on the right depending on how much you are prepared to pay for a click, as well as how well you've set your campaign up – more on that later.

What Google Wants

However, before you even begin to create your account it is important you fully understand what you are getting into. Many people make the mistake of believing that Google and Google AdWords is there purely to make them sales... it's not. Whilst Google is potentially helping you make money, it also wants to make a tidy sum for itself. This does not mean that you and Google are working against each other; in fact you actually want quite similar things. But the best way to think of AdWords is simply as an intermediary between you - the seller, and the searcher (your potential customer). Google is simply another marketing channel – a very effective channel nonetheless.

Google's loyalties lie with the searcher as they have realised that the key to being the number one search engine is to provide the best results when someone searches, so they keep coming back. It is the searchers that make Google money; advertisers will pay Google to get in front of Google's valuable searchers.

This is where you come in.

Now, Google didn't get to the top by chance. They have spent years perfecting their search engine to bring up the most relevant results for anyone searching on Google. As a result they have a reputation to uphold and so its standards are very high. Google will not display adverts unless they are relevant enough for the searcher to click. Remember, Google wants their searchers to get the answer, come back to Google time and time again, so that Google can keep making money. Currently 93%[3] of Google's profits come from Google AdWords, so they must be doing something right!

What You Want

There are a number of reasons why advertisers choose to use Google AdWords and below are some of the more common ones:
- Adding online retail
- Wanting more traffic

- Wanting a reliable source of leads and sales
- Quick and easy way of advertising

The list goes on. While all of these reasons are perfectly valid it all comes down to one thing, profitable advertising. People use Google AdWords to make money.

Whilst on the surface your aims and the aims of Google appear to be poles apart, they are more similar than you would think. You both want RELEVANCY. Google wants your adverts to be relevant so people click on them and then get what they want, whilst YOU want your adverts to be relevant so that when someone does click on your ad, they find what they are looking for and make either a further enquiry about your product or service, or make a purchase.

Making Google AdWords Work for You

As a small business owner you probably look at the multinational corporation that is Google which hosts adverts from other multinational companies and think... no thanks! But you're wrong, it can be done. Yes, it may be daunting, but there are many ways in which even the smallest companies can successfully compete with the giants, generating quality leads and sales. As you may have already guessed, that is pretty much what this whole book is about, but here are three ways in which you as a seller can make a profit from Google AdWords.

1) **Find a niche.** If you are competing in a market with tonnes of companies, all of whom are big and powerful, chances are they will out bid you every time. BUT if you find an area to specialise, in which they do not feature, then you're onto a winner!
2) **Location, location, location.** Location targeting is a great way of refining your search to ensure that the people who click on your advert will be able to use your product or service successfully. For example, if you're a removals company operating in and around Blackpool, you don't want a searcher from London clicking on your advert and wasting your money, unless of course the Londoner is moving to Blackpool.
3) **Relevancy.** Yes I know I've talked about this already, but it is just SO important. If your advert is relevant and includes good

information, if your landing page is what the searcher is expecting based on your advert and the location settings are right, then not only are you more likely to be shown on page one of Google, but you are also more likely to get leads and sales (conversions) from your clicks!

Go On, Take The Plunge…

AdWords may seem like a big leap for a small business to make, but with many small businesses successfully using AdWords to grow, doesn't it make sense to join today! So stop wasting time dithering about whether it is the right move for you, your competitors are most likely on AdWords already. Get started right away, put your company on to the first page of Google using Google AdWords, and get those crucial leads and sales to boost your company's success.

Rapid Recap:

- You don't have to be a computer 'wizz', a finance expert or a company with money to burn, as this book will go on to make abundantly clear, AdWords is for pretty much everyone.
- There are multiple advantages you can gain from using AdWords; be it the ability to sell more online, to increase your customer base or simply to increase the accessibility of your business.
- To dominate on AdWords, you need to remember three key things; find a niche, be specific on location and be relevant!
- The best way to find out if it can work for you is to try it.

Chapter Two
Your business – Are you ready?

<u>Defining Both Yourself and Your Customer</u>
In the previous chapter I focused on helping you understand Google's role in the online marketing process and what they want from you as a seller/advertiser. Now you fully understand the who's, what's, where's and why's of Google, it's your turn.

Before you even begin to take the plunge into the world of AdWords you must first take a good, long hard look at yourself and decide who you are as a company. Now I know that may sound ridiculous and a cliché, but seriously, before you create your first campaign you must know EXACTLY what your business is about and what it is aiming to achieve using AdWords. If you don't, you could end up wasting a lot of time, energy and money.

In simple terms, if you don't know exactly who your target market is, it makes it almost impossible to find out what makes them tick.

One of the factors which will affect how you choose to use AdWords is the activity of your competitors, so take the time to do a little research in your sector. See who is active on AdWords; what are they selling, do they appear to be successful, are there several companies which appear to dominate in your sector? For the small business owner, doing this research to find the answers to these questions is vital to your success. As I've already said there is often no point in trying to compete with the superpowers of the internet world head on, so instead look at what they are not offering. Find your niche before you start on your quest with Google AdWords. Finding a niche is equivalent to finding a direction and without a direction you'll find yourself going nowhere. There are plenty of examples of small companies who have found a niche in their market and used Google AdWords to help them dominate it.

Take the successful insurance company Butler Evans, a client of mine for many years. Butler Evans offers a range of business insurance services for small and medium size businesses. Obviously this market is extremely competitive and so when competing with huge insurance companies; smaller companies such as Butler Evans barely get a look in. So they've done the opposite, they've chosen not to compete. Now by this I don't mean they've pulled out all together, (it's not that easy!) but rather they are targeting their customers from a different angle. Instead of using keywords such as 'business insurance' or even 'professional indemnity insurance' they are targeting even more specific niches like 'professional indemnity insurance specifically for solicitors' and 'insurance specifically for waste management companies'. By targeting particular sectors and by using specific keywords, they are attracting the right customers for their specific products; they are seen as experts in that particular sector and as a result secure above average leads and sales for these specialist sectors or niches. Once they have the customer they also offer the other more general insurance services as well - success.

At this point you may well be thinking, "Sure, find a niche, but how?" Firstly, think about your strengths; what do you or could you excel at and where are you making the most sales and profits. Secondly and perhaps more importantly, ask your current customers. Ask them key questions like:

1. **Why do you buy from us?** What makes us different compared to others that offer the same or a similar product or service? What makes us different?
2. **What would you key into Google if you were looking for someone like us?** How do you describe our product or service? You could look at emails from your prospects and clients to see how they describe you too.
3. **When you key in the product or service you are looking for, how easy is it to find the answer or solution?** If it is difficult, or there seems to be fewer competitors, then you may well have found your niche!

Another way is to look at it like Butler Evans and pick specific niches or alternatively promote part of what you offer that could start a conversation with the right sort of companies, which could then lead to sales of your main products and services, or additional products or services.

Piab Ltd provides vacuum solutions for automated material handling for businesses, and is another client of mine, who has successfully used Google AdWords to promote one specific part of their vast product range. Thinking both strategically and tactically they decided to target a product that is required; is a consumable and isn't too expensive; the suction cup product. It is commonly used on packaging machines, pick and placement and production machinery, so using suction cups means Piab can start a conversation with a potential client, which can lead to purchases of suction cups, as well as further purchases of vacuum pumps and other accessories.

You have to think imaginatively about what you have to offer. Perhaps promote just one element of the full range or maybe decide on one sector that you know you can excel in and show those potential customers that you have expertise and knowledge in their particular niche.

Doing this upfront research won't just help to make your potential AdWords campaign a success; it will also help the rest of your marketing effort too. You can use what you have identified in your other marketing activities, whether that's email, direct mail or PR. So do this research!

Are You Ready?
Now you've established your direction you need to check everything else is in order before you get started. Here's a mini checklist of all the things you'll certainly need - they're all pretty basic but without them, you're going nowhere.
You will need:
- A domain name
- A website for your company
- A shopping cart linked to your website (if you're going to be selling online)
- And obviously, you'll need a product or service to sell

To register a domain name, simply Google 'domain name registration' and you'll find plenty of companies offering domain name registration facilities as well as ways to get your site up and running.

Obviously, your website is crucial. It needs to provide the visitor with right information and make it obvious what options they have in terms of the next step. This is where your potential customer will go to browse through your products and perhaps make a purchase. It's your shop window as well as your store. There is no point working hard on getting your website to the top of page 1 of Google if the website doesn't give the right impression. If it's poorly laid out and makes it difficult for the visitor to know what to do, it's more likely that your potential customer will move their cursor straight to that back button, therefore wasting a valuable click as well as money – remember with Google, you 'pay per click'.

Compare your website with your competitors; does your website need a revamp before you start spending with Google?

This takes us onto the next point; if you're selling online you need a shopping cart, no cart, no sales; it's as simple as that. Well almost, you also need to make sure the process of buying from you is quick, easy and straightforward. Test it for yourself before you start promoting your product or service. Ask others to test it for you and if necessary simplify the process.

Before you start spending with Google you'll also want to make sure you can track what is happening; enquiries, downloads and sales can easily be tracked. The more tracking you implement the better as it will help you to understand what is happening so you can optimise the AdWords campaigns you've set up with accurate data. I will show you how to set it up in chapter 7. And last but certainly not least, you need your product or service to stand out from the crowd.

<u>Understanding the Lifetime Value of Your Customer</u>
Okay so you've found your niche, you've sorted all the bits and bobs for your online campaign, now there's just one final thing to consider before you get going… THE BUDGET. Two dreaded words that strike fear into the hearts of many small business owners when it comes to online marketing. Just how much should you spend? How much is too much? How little is too little?

Okay, forget the money for a second. The big question is… Are you in it to win it? Of course the answer should be yes!

There are plenty of tactics and tricks which can really help to keep your costs on AdWords down. BUT (and I can't stress this enough) it is important to recognise, just as you would when it comes to any other form of marketing, the rule of thumb when it comes to advertising… those who pay the most often get the most in return - first winning and then keeping the customer.

Whilst investing that extra pound or two may seem like an expensive gamble, the profit which you will receive from investing that extra money will often comeback threefold, fourfold or even more. In this case, it is vital to think of the **lifetime value of the customer** – what you spend on getting them now; they will spend that and more with you tomorrow and in the future. It is important that you calculate the lifetime value of the customer as it gives you a much better idea of how much you can afford to spend getting a customer.

The basic formula is:

(Average Value of a Sale) X (Number of Repeat Transactions) X (Average Retention Time in Months or Years for a Typical Customer)
(See Brad Sugars article http://www.entrepreneur.com/article/224153)

An example would be the lifetime value of a beauty salon visitor or member who spends £60 every month for three years. The salon owner knows that she can expect to keep a customer for, on average, three years. The value of that customer would be:

£60 X (12 months X 3 years) = £2,160 in total revenue (or £720 per year)

So you can see even from this example why many salon owners offer a free or reduced first treatment to help drive traffic. This salon owner knows that as long as they spend less than £720 to acquire a new customer, the customer will prove profitable as long as the salon owner keeps them for more than a year.

And don't forget, one of the great advantages with Google AdWords is you can set a daily budget which Google won't exceed in a given month, based on a month being 30.4 days. So you know the maximum you'll be spending each month with Google.

For example £10 per day = £10 x 30.4 days = £304 for the month.

In the salon owner example above, if they can get at least one customer per month from their Google AdWords activity, spending £20 per day, they will have got that customer profitably.

So before you start, do some simple maths and work out just how much you can spend getting a customer.

Rapid Recap
- Customer research is absolutely essential for every business owner, not just the small business owner, wanting to use Google AdWords. To give the customer what they want, you need to know what that is!
- Make sure you and your business are totally ready for AdWords and any potential influx of enquiries and customers. There is no point beginning the AdWords process unless you can tick all the boxes, so ensure you have a domain, website and shopping cart ready to go.
- Understanding the lifetime value of the customer is crucial to using AdWords. What you put into getting the customer can come back to you when they become a customer.

CHAPTER THREE
KEYWORD RESEARCH

So now you have established exactly what you want from Google AdWords, it's time to take it to the next level and create a list of keywords. In case you're unsure; keywords are the phrases which you input into your campaign, which if someone typed into Google would trigger your advert to be displayed. So for example; "oven cleaning Nottingham" or "letting agent Mansfield" would trigger your advert if you were targeting those phrases.

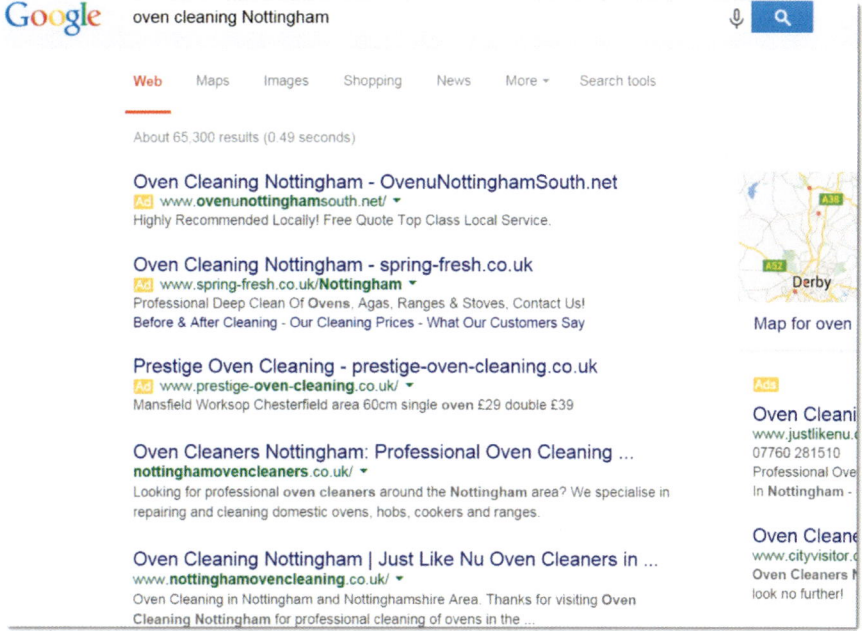

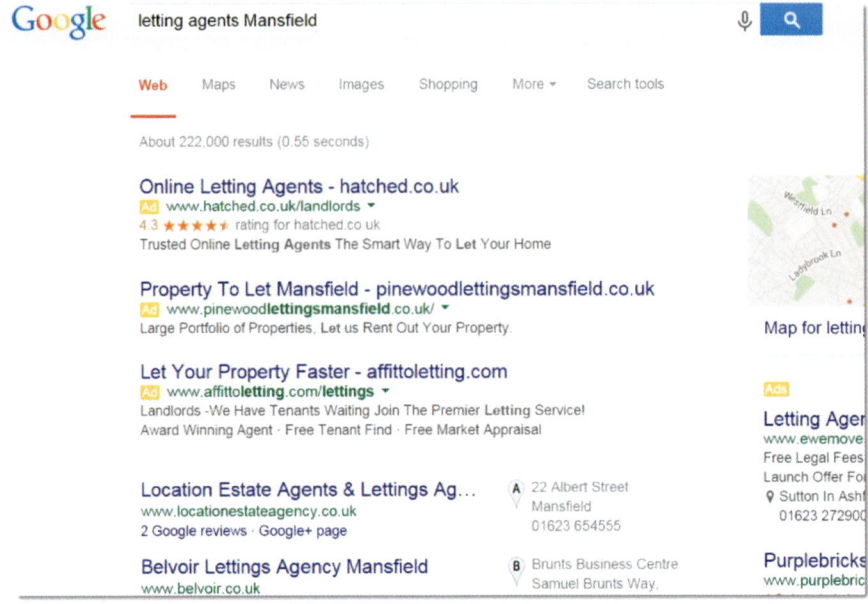

Your keywords form the very foundation of your campaign; if this foundation is weak your entire campaign will be less effective. It is so important to have the right keywords to get the right people to click on your advert and make that purchase.

Just think about how many people go to Google looking for something to buy or to find the answer to a question. What they type into the search bar is their way of trying to solve their issue, whatever that may be. Their search will contain keywords and the keywords will vary for most searchers. It is your job as a small business owner to suss out the keywords that are relevant to your company and the products or services you wish to promote using Google AdWords. If you add a comprehensive list to your campaign, it is more likely that you will get more clicks and that these clicks will be from people who actually will want what you offer.

Identifying Your Customers Before Your Keywords
Before you begin the process of identifying keywords, it's important to understand the types of customers who are on the web and may see your advert. Internet marketers generally agree that there are three categories of searcher and it is vital that you understand the difference between them before deciding on the keywords to include in your campaign.

GROUP 1: **The Browser**. We all do it; aimless browsing of the web, not really looking for anything in particular other than to fill time, be it as a distraction from work, waiting to pick up the kids from school or when using public transport trying to avoid the gaze of the person opposite you. These people are not really who you are looking to target with your advert, as it is unlikely that browsing will turn to buying; certainly not immediately.

TIP: For the small business owner with a budget in mind, you can waste a lot of budget with the Browser so you're actually best avoiding them.

GROUP 2: **The Shopper**. Now this group of people are more selective than the previous, they have something in mind but they're not exactly sure what it is yet. Say, they want a new camera; they know they'd like a Nikon, they know they want it to be black but that's about it. These people are still researching their potential purchase and so can be 'hit and miss'; some will research and turn to buying, others will research and decide against it.

GROUP 3: **The Buyer**. Payment at the ready, they know what they want; they just need to find the place to buy. This, ladies and gentleman, is your captive audience. This is the key group which you need to tap into to get those leads and sales for your business.

To identify which category a searcher is in is fairly easy. Someone who is simply 'browsing' isn't going to type into the search bar 'buy Nikon d3200'- that is far too specific. However, this IS the type of keyword phrase which would be entered by a 'buyer'. This is why as an AdWords beginner and for most small businesses, *Group 3* is the group you need to be targeting as this is the group who are most likely to become your customers. Once your campaign is up and running and successful, then you may be able to turn your attention to the 'shoppers' and potentially the 'browsers', but for now forget those people and focus on those eagerly scanning the web to make a purchase.

Finding Your Keywords
Okay so how do you actually find these enticing phrases and words which you want to be found for on Google? Well, I have created a super simple flow diagram which step by step takes you through the process you need to follow

in order to create your list, it couldn't be easier!

#1. What is your product or service?

It's painfully obvious but it has to be said, if you're a company selling dishwashers, then 'buy dishwashers' would probably be one of your keywords you would use.

#2. Who else is out there?

As I've said before, it is vital to be aware of your competition. Type in on Google your potential keyword and see who comes up.

TIP: Check out what Google provides as alternatives with Google Instant (as you type in the phrase more options are provided as shown below) and related searches are shown at the bottom of the Google results page too.

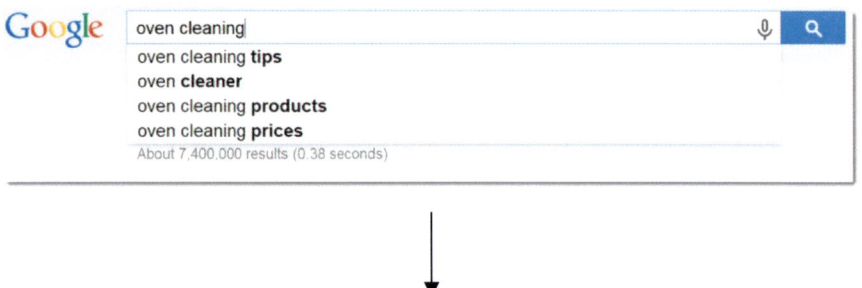

#3. What does the customer want?

Don't know? Ask them – in fact ask them even if you think you know! Go to clients and quiz them on how they came to find you. Ask them what they would type into Google if they were to try and find you now.

TIP: Look back at emails from customers to see how they describe what you offer.

#4. Build your list

After you've established the answers to the above, you should start building your list. So open up an excel document and begin entering in your options. This exercise will get a little repetitive but that's the point, try and think of as many variations of your keywords as you can, even if it's just one word in a phrase that you're changing.

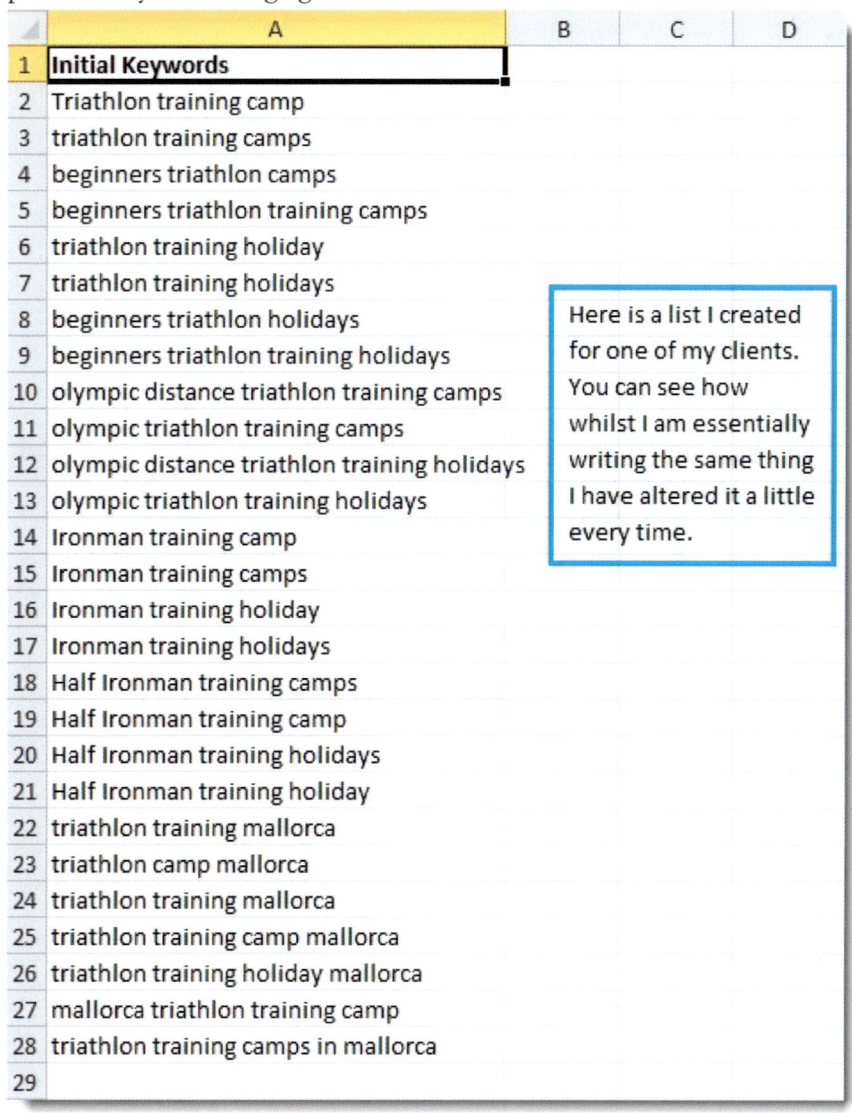

Here is a list I created for one of my clients. You can see how whilst I am essentially writing the same thing I have altered it a little every time.

You need to try and cover every possible search term for your product or service. Look at how you describe it on your website as well as how your competitors describe it on theirs.

TIP: Always include at least two words in your keywords/phrases.

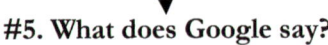

#5. What does Google say?

After all, it's Google who will be hosting your advert, so it's definitely a good idea to check out their free Keyword Planner tool to see their recommendations.

<u>Using Google's Keyword Planner</u>

As I said in #5, before you add your keywords to your Google AdWords campaign, it's worth giving Google's free tool; the Keyword Planner a try to see the extra words it can add to your list.

So go to your AdWords account, go to 'Tools' and select the 'Keyword Planner' option in the drop down menu. (There's information on setting up your AdWords account available in Chapter 4.)

TIP: To help build your negatives list, the Keyword Planner is a vital step in the process.

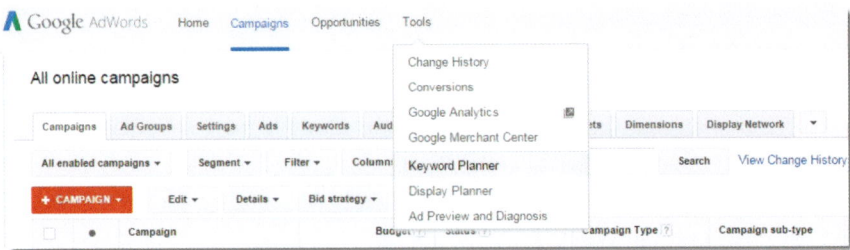

You will then be presented with four options; different actions you can perform using the Keyword Planner. Select the top option 'Search for new keywords and ad group ideas'.

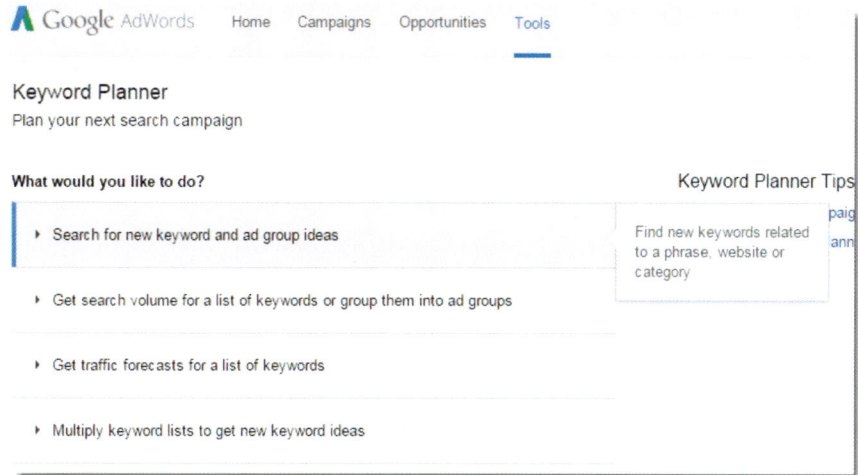

Now you have the opportunity to enter the list of keywords you have come up with in to the top box, this gives Google something to work from. You needn't worry about filling in the next two boxes about your landing page or product category. Edit the targeting settings to suit your needs. For most of you; you won't need to change anything. Once you've done this, click 'Get Ideas'.

Google will now have given you a massive list of both Ad Group ideas and keyword ideas. The page which has appeared probably seems quite daunting with its graph and table, but don't freak out, simply make sure you are on the 'Keyword ideas' tab and click the 'Download button' at the top right corner of the list.

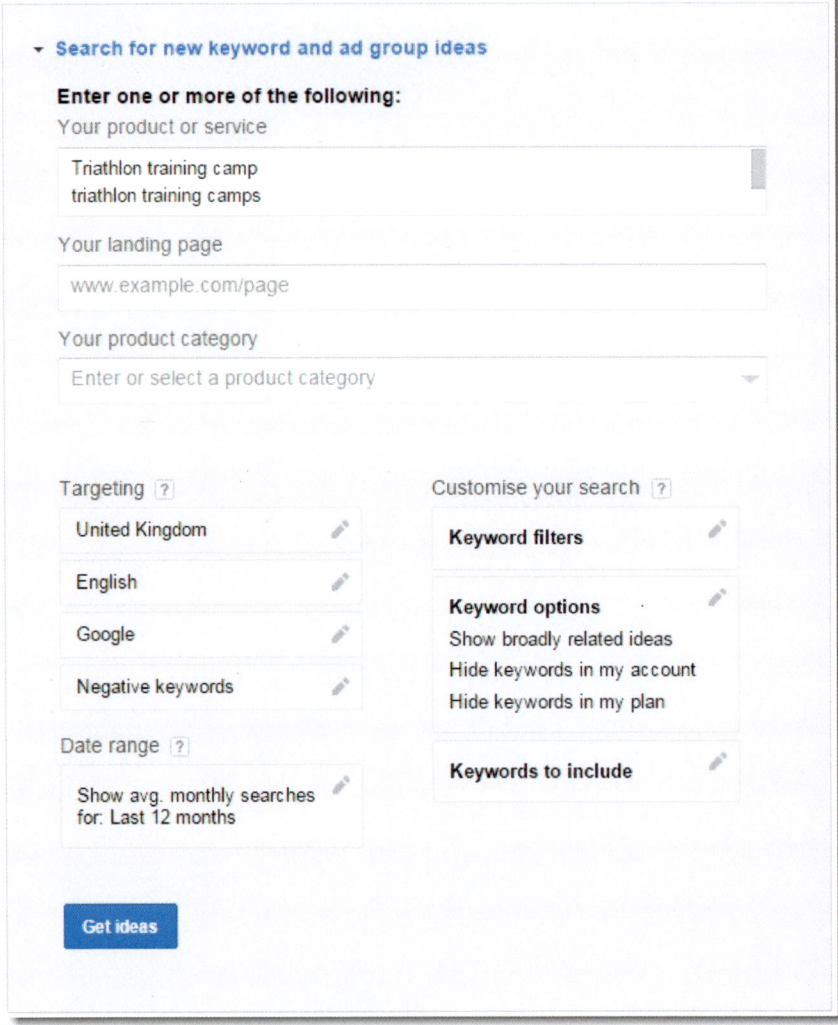

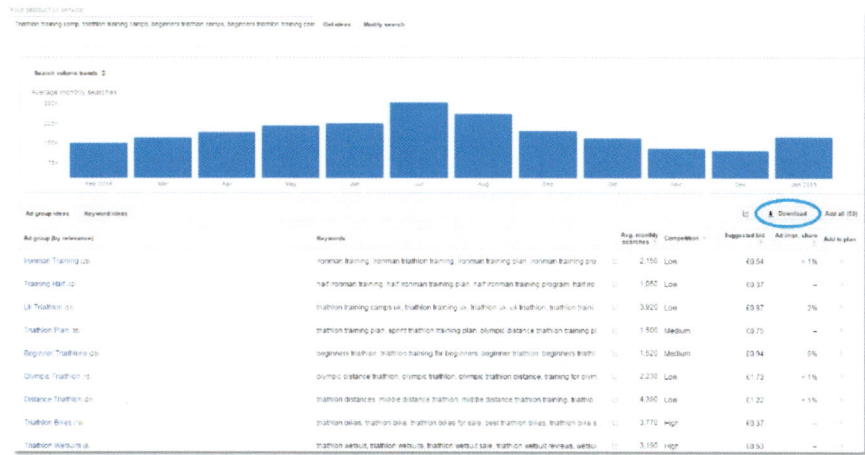

The Download page is shown in close up below.

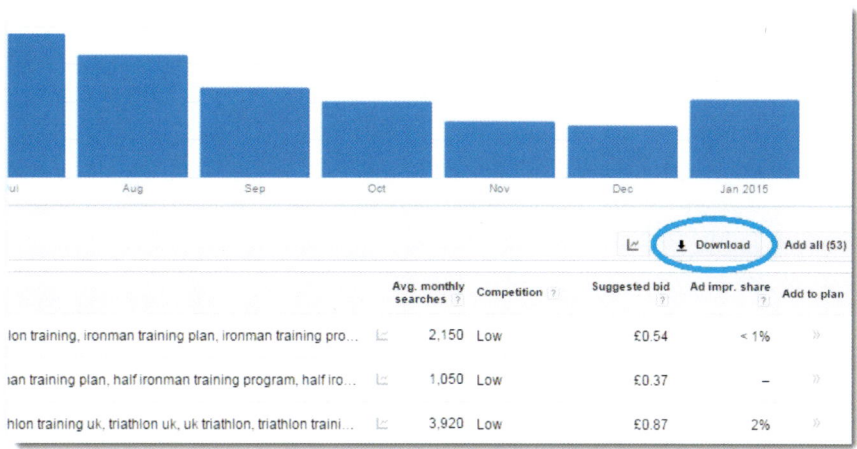

You'll need to click Download again when the instruction pops up and then Save File when that appears. Google will now download all its ideas into excel for you.

It is now your job to complete the painstaking task of going through them and picking out the ones you want. Yes, this may seem like a chore but it really needs to be done. As you go through the options don't simply discard the ones you don't want and keep the ones you do, think about categorising them into different groups as this will save you time further down the line.

So create new tabs on your excel document and place all similar keywords on particular sheets. See my example excel document below.

Most importantly during this process you also want to identify and create a list of your Negative keywords. These are the phrases you don't want to be found for and Google's long list will help you to identify some of them.

TIP: If you don't want to include a phrase, does a word in the phrase, or the phrase, or part of the phrase need to be a Negative? This is a great way to build your Negative list and it will save you significant money if you are thorough in your work at this point.

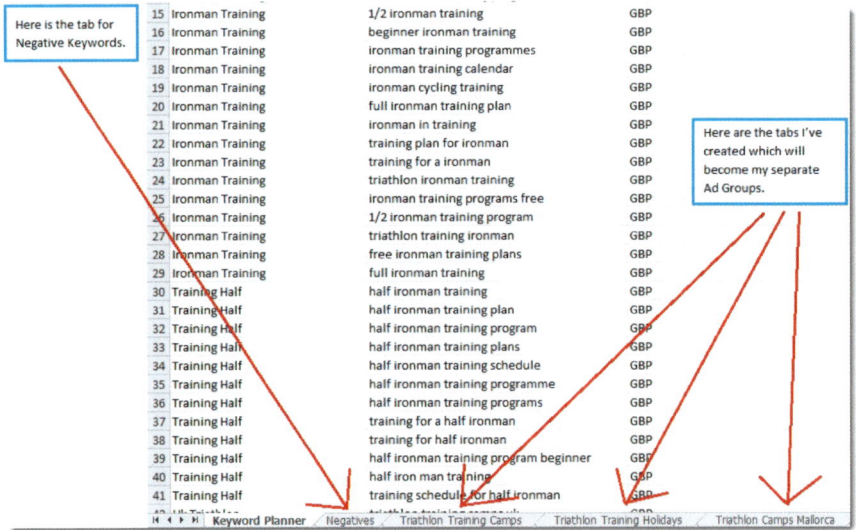

Grouping Your Keywords
If you do your keyword research properly you'll find that you'll have a wide variety of keywords which although are all linked to your product or service, aren't that similar. If you can you should group together your keywords which are most similar to each other and allocate them to a specific Ad Group. You will then have several Ad Groups which although they may target the same product or service, will describe it in slightly different ways. You are effectively putting your keywords into themes.

For example, if you are a Maths Tutor providing Maths courses you may want your keywords to cover the variety of services you offer, so you would set out up your campaigns and Ad Groups up like this:

1)	Maths Course Online	(Campaign)
i.	Maths Lessons Online Nottingham	(Ad Group)
ii.	Maths Tutorials Online Nottingham	(Ad Group)
iii.	Maths Video Course Online Nottingham	(Ad Group)
2)	Maths Course At Home	(Campaign)
i.	Maths Course At Home Nottingham	(Ad Group)
ii.	Maths Course 1-to-1 Nottingham	(Ad Group)
3)	Group Maths Courses	(Campaign)
i.	Maths Centre Nottingham	(Ad Group)
ii.	Maths Group Learning Nottingham	(Ad Group)
iii.	Maths Class Nottingham	(Ad Group)

<u>Different Types of Keywords</u>
Beware. Many people think that once you have found your list of keywords all you have to do is input them into your AdWords account and hey presto, you're onto a winner. This is definitely **not** the case. Before you enter your list into your campaign there is one more thing which you must do in order to make sure you make the Google AdWords system work for you, or else all that research you've done to find your keywords will have been for nothing.

Google, in case you hadn't realised, is pretty clever and so not only can you select specific keywords, but you can also dictate what type of 'match' has to occur with your keywords for your ad to be shown (or not shown) on Google. To do this Google has formulated five types of keywords, these are... Broad, Broad Match Modified, Phrase, Exact and Negative (used to stop your ads from showing) keywords.

1) Broad
This is the most unspecific 'broad' way to enter your keywords. While your ad may appear lots and you may get lots of clicks, this is often NOT a good thing. By not specifying how you want your keyword to be matched to what is typed into Google, your ad could appear for things almost completely

unrelated to your product or service.

For example; let's say you are selling high quality second hand cars. One of your keywords could simply be

Quality Second Hand Cars

Yes, the keyword does indeed reflect the product you're hoping to sell but it is likely that your ad will not just appear to those looking to purchase a *quality* second hand car but also search terms such as,

"Budget Second Hand Cars" (unless you've added budget as a negative in the campaign of course)

Whilst the majority of the words match, there is a crucial element which does not; the price range. If you are looking to sell more upmarket cars, someone looking for a 'budget' buy is not your ideal customer. This is where first time users of AdWords regularly come unstuck. It is very important to stop your ad from appearing in searches made by people who won't be interested in making a purchase from you at all. All you will be doing is wasting a great deal of money.

2) Broad Match Modified

This is the next step up, by simply using the + sign your campaigns can suddenly become a lot more effective. By putting a + in front of one or more words, you tell Google that this word (or close variations including misspellings, singular/plural forms, abbreviations and acronyms, and stemmings such as "fish" and "fishing") need to be in the words entered by the searcher.

So using the same example, if you were to input

+Quality +Second +Hand +Cars

It is far more likely that your advert will appear for relevant searches, as the word 'quality', or variations of it, will always appear.

TIP: I generally include a + sign before every word as you have more control by doing this.

3) Phrase Match

This time enter your keyword with speech marks either side of it. So for our example it would be,

"Quality Second Hand Cars"

This ensures that your advert will only appear if the phrase keyed into Google's search bar contains all the keywords that you have specified, or close variations of them, with potentially with extra words included before or after the keywords you have specified.

4) Exact Match

Last but certainly not least is the most precise matching of all. Exact match is the least likely to get you unnecessary clicks, all through the use of square brackets before and after the phrase. So taking the same keyword, you would input:

[Quality Second Hand Cars]

In this case, the only time your advert would appear would be if that exact phrase were to be entered into the Google search bar.

5) Negative Keywords

Negative keywords are simply words or phrases which if you input into the correct box in AdWords, Google will ensure that when these keywords are entered into Google, your advert will NOT appear. It really is amazing how many random searches will trigger your advert to appear when it's just not relevant. The above scenario is a prime example of where using Negative keywords will really save you money. By including words like 'cheap', 'free' and 'budget' in your list of Negatives you'll eliminate a whole range of people who aren't suited for what you're trying to sell, therefore saving yourself a whole load of clicks and potentially loads of money. Simple yet effective and so often missed by newbies to Google AdWords. (For further examples of negative keywords, check out our list at the back of this book.)

TIP: Google won't prompt you to add your Negatives so you have to remember to add them.

TIP: I recommend NOT using Broad altogether as it is just too vague and can lead to far too many unwanted clicks. It is so easy for your budget to be spent very quickly and for all the wrong types of searches. If you want to keep it simple, I'd recommend using Broad Match Modified and potentially Exact. And always add Negatives before you set your campaign live.

So there you have it. Yes, keywords may not be the most interesting feature of AdWords, but they are absolutely paramount when it comes to ensuring that you get the clicks you want whilst not wasting money on clicks you really don't need. So no matter how much you are tempted to skip over it quickly, take the time to develop your long list of keywords, and go through the even longer list provided by Google's Keyword Planner. Trust me, you won't regret it.

Rapid Recap

- Keywords form the basis of your campaign, but to build your list of keywords you'll need to do some research into your product or service and use the free tool provided by Google; the Keyword Planner to create a truly comprehensive list.
- There are several different types of keyword each with their own symbol, which you need to add to your keywords before adding them to Google AdWords to make your campaign a success.
  -Broad Match Modified using + eg. +Your +Keywords
  -Phrase Match using speech marks eg. "Your Keywords"
  -Exact Match by using [ ] e.g. [Your Keywords]
  By using these you have more control than just using Broad (which I've seen many a business owner use).
- Negative keywords are the words which you do not want to be found for. Create a list of Negative keywords and input them into your AdWords campaign to reduce unnecessary clicks. Check out our negative keyword list in the back of this book for some useful ideas. I can't stress enough the importance of Negative keywords as using these ensures your Ad will only appear when you want it to. Negative keywords, quite simply, save you money. Again many business owners either aren't aware or don't use them – if you do, you'll be a step ahead of some of your competitors for sure.

TIP: Want a quick and easy way of getting your keywords into the various match types? You can download a useful spreadsheet to help with this at www.jackie-key.com/keywordmatch

Chapter Checklist
Using the Keyword Planner
- ✓ Select 'Tools' at the top of AdWords and click on 'Keyword Planner'.
- ✓ Select 'Search for new keyword and ad group ideas'.
- ✓ Enter your list of keywords and edit settings if needed. Click 'Get Ideas'.
- ✓ Make sure you are on the 'Keyword ideas' tab and click download.
- ✓ When the pop up box appears, select download again and 'save file'. It will now be downloaded into an excel spreadsheet.
- ✓ Go through keywords and eliminate unwanted suggestions – consider whether they are also negatives.
- ✓ Start grouping keywords into Ad Groups using different tabs in an excel document, including a tab for negative keywords.
- ✓ Edit to include Broad Match Modified and potentially Exact (the others aren't that useful these days).

CHAPTER FOUR
ADWORDS CAMPAIGN SET UP

This chapter is going to take you through how to create your AdWords account, a campaign, an Ad Group and an advert. Before we begin however, it's important that you get to grips with the structure of your account so you fully understand how it works.

The Structure of AdWords

If you're a total newcomer to AdWords, getting your head round the structure is one of the first things you need to do. I have found that's it's best to see AdWords as a tiered system, similar to a family tree! To start you have your account, within your account you have your campaigns, within each campaign you have Ad Groups and within the Ad Groups you have your adverts and keywords.

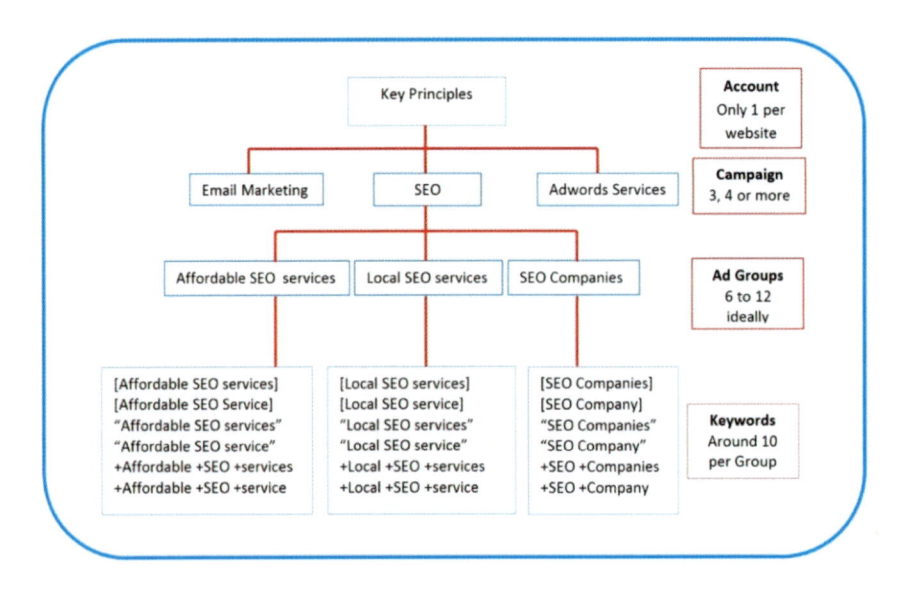

Key Principles	**Account** — Only 1 per website
Email Marketing / SEO / Adwords Services	**Campaign** — 3, 4 or more
Affordable SEO services / Local SEO services / SEO Companies	**Ad Groups** — 6 to 12 ideally
[Affordable SEO services] / [Affordable SEO Service] / "Affordable SEO services" / "Affordable SEO service" / +Affordable +SEO +services / +Affordable +SEO +service [Local SEO services] / [Local SEO service] / "Local SEO services" / "Local SEO service" / +Local +SEO +services / +Local +SEO +service [SEO Companies] / [SEO Company] / "SEO Companies" / "SEO Company" / +SEO +Companies / +SEO +Company	**Keywords** — Around 10 per Group

As you can see from the above example I have only developed the central campaign 'SEO'. Of course in a real account, you would go on to develop the other campaigns 'Email Marketing' and 'AdWords Services' in a similar way.

Google has recently changed their settings so that instead of setting up your account and then setting up a campaign and then an Ad Group you do it pretty much all at once. So if you've already got an account and are simply looking to create another campaign skip through to the section 'Setting Up More Campaigns'.

For those wanting to set up an AdWords account, please take a look at the next section.

Creating an Account

To get started, you can simply 'Google', 'Google AdWords' and you'll find a link to setting up an account.

When it comes to entering the settings for your account, Google has broken down the process into four steps:

✓ About your business   ② Your first campaign   ③ Billing   ④ Review

I'm going to follow this structure as I explain what you need to do.

1.0 About Your Business
1.1 Email and web address

The first thing you'll be asked for is an email address and your website address.

TIP: Use same email as your Google Analytics account if you have one. Make sure it is an email address you have access to as you may need to verify it at the end.

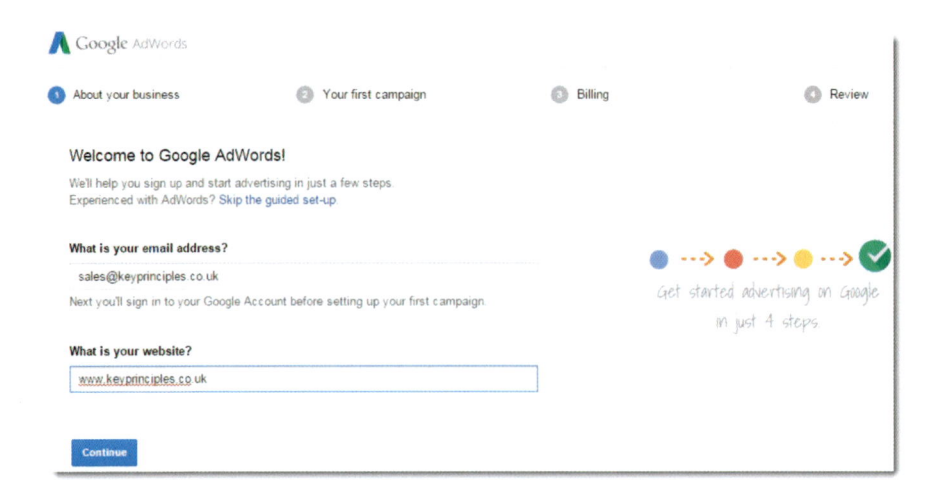

Google AdWords

| 1 About your business | 2 Your first campaign | 3 Billing | 4 Review |

Welcome to Google AdWords!

We'll help you sign up and start advertising in just a few steps.
Experienced with AdWords? Skip the guided set-up.

What is your email address?

sales@keyprinciples.co.uk

Next you'll sign in to your Google Account before setting up your first campaign.

What is your website?

www.keyprinciples.co.uk

[Continue]

Get started advertising on Google in just 4 steps.

1.2 Create Google Account

To create the account, you'll need to add the following information to the 'About Your Business' page:

>Name
>Email
>Password
>Date of Birth
>Mobile Number
>Enter the verification code

Clicking next step brings you to 'Your first campaign' page.

2.0 Your First Campaign

Don't worry too much when filling in this page as once it's completed you can pause your campaign and either create a new one or edit the one created.

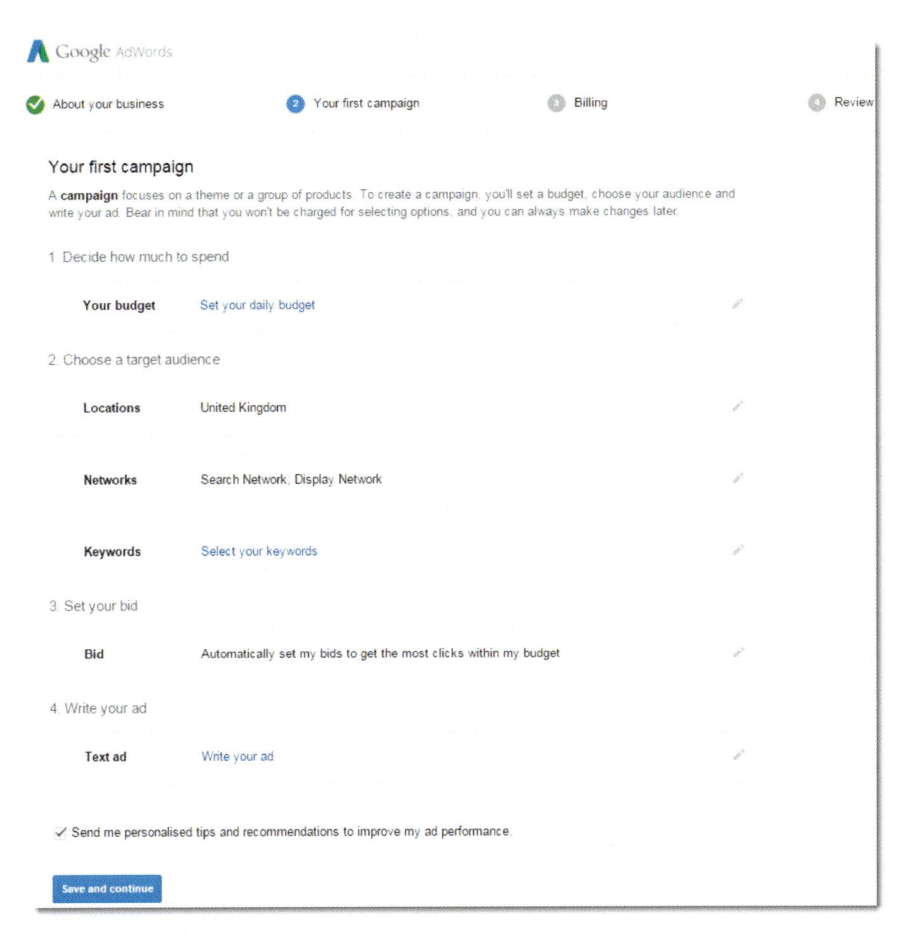

Here you need to:

2.1 Decide how much to spend. Whilst this completely depends on your business and how much you can afford to spend, I'd recommend setting your budget to around £10 per day initially.

2.2 Choose a target audience; this includes Location, Networks and Keywords.

    a) **Location.** Type in the location you want to target. In England this could be the country, county, city or town and in the USA it could be a state, city or town.

    b) **Networks.** You need to change from the automated selection of 'Display Network' and switch to 'Search Network' as shown in the image below. **Untick the 'Display Network' box.**

TIP: Even though Google suggests it, never run Search and Display campaigns together. Keep them separate for maximum control.

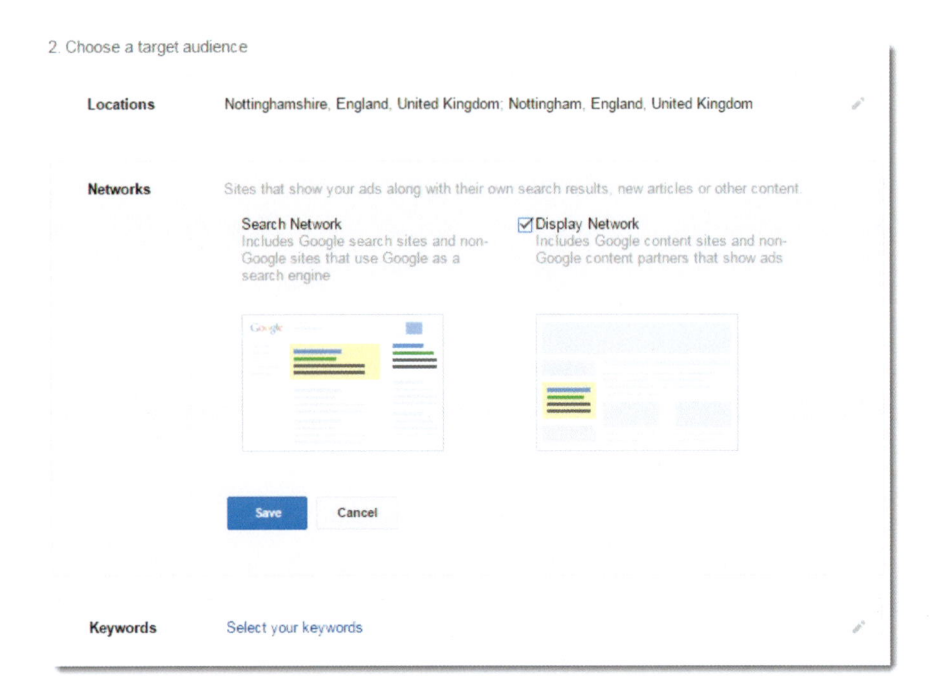

c) **Keywords.** Add in some initial keywords – Google provides suggestions based on your website address which may or may not be 'helpful' and may appear to be 'Broad' – the sort of match type I wouldn't recommend!

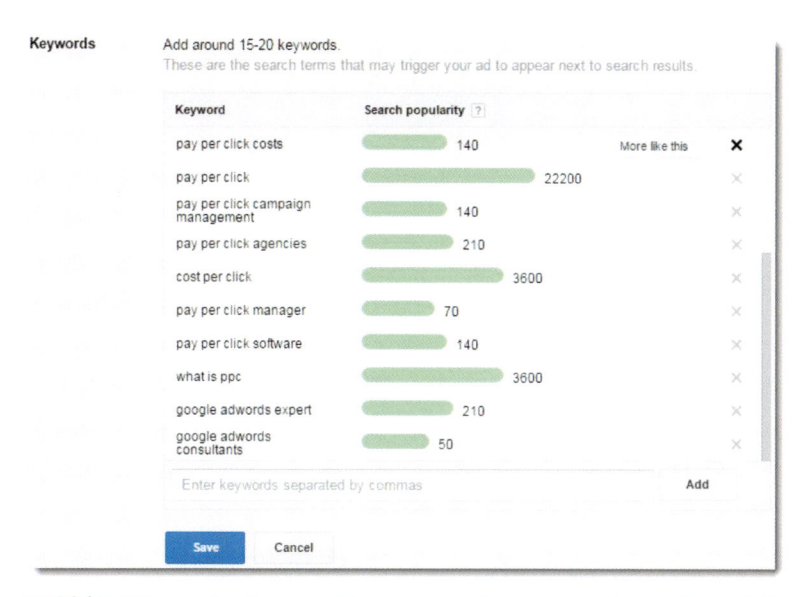

Keyword	Search popularity	
pay per click costs	140	More like this ✕
pay per click	22200	✕
pay per click campaign management	140	✕
pay per click agencies	210	✕
cost per click	3600	✕
pay per click manager	70	✕
pay per click software	140	✕
what is ppc	3600	✕
google adwords expert	210	✕
google adwords consultants	50	✕

NOTE: If you don't actually remove the suggestions, they will be included in your first campaign and Ad Group! So I would recommend 'crossing out' all the suggestions and adding a couple of relevant ones instead!

2.3 **Set a Bid** – interestingly Google's default is 'automatically set my bids'. This is not recommended unless you want Google to have control, so change to 'I'll set my bid manually'.

2.4 **Write Your Text Ad** – note that the landing page will be your home address unless you change it! I'd recommend that in most cases you change it to the most relevant page on your website. There's plenty of information on writing your advert in Chapter 5, but in the meantime just fill in the information and you can review it, or pause it, at the end of this initial set up.

4. Write your ad

Text ad Landing page
http://www.keyprinciples.co.uk

Ad

Headline

www.keyprinciples.co.uk

Ad text

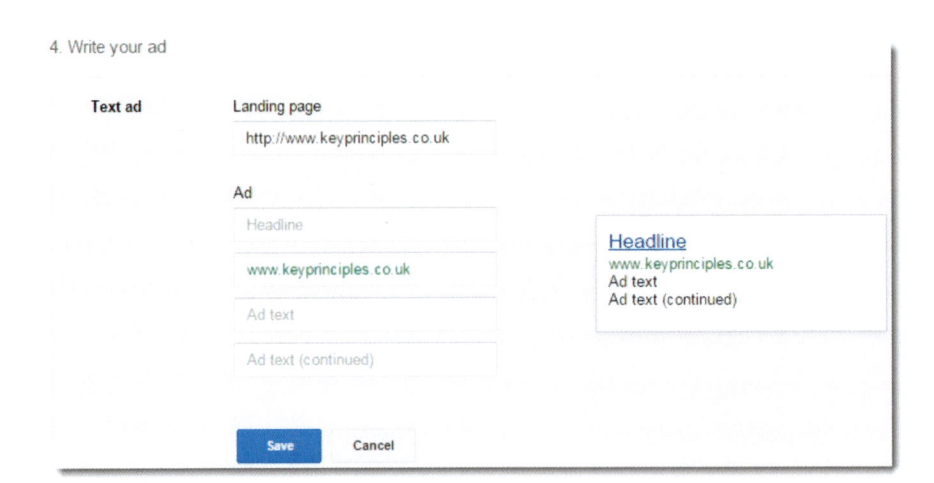

Ad text (continued)

Headline
www.keyprinciples.co.uk
Ad text
Ad text (continued)

Save   Cancel

Your completed campaign should look something like the screenshot on page 37:

Press 'Save and continue' and you come to the Billing Screen which you need to complete.

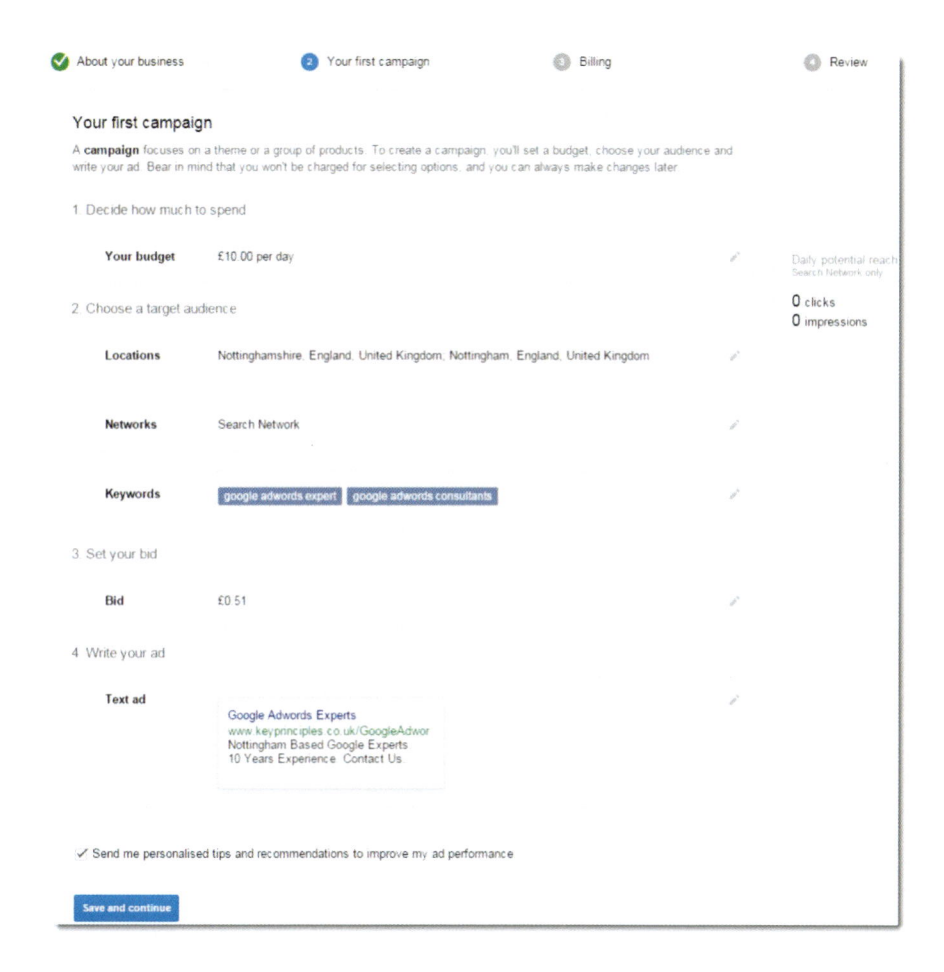

3.0 Billing

Simply fill in the details requested. As part of the billing process you'll be prompted to provide an introductory offer code. If you don't have one, then get one from me! Simply email hello@jackie-key.com and if I've got a spare introductory code, I'll email it to you.

In the UK, also note that you will want to change the time zone to GMT London rather than the default of GMT (No daylight saving).

Click 'Save and continue'

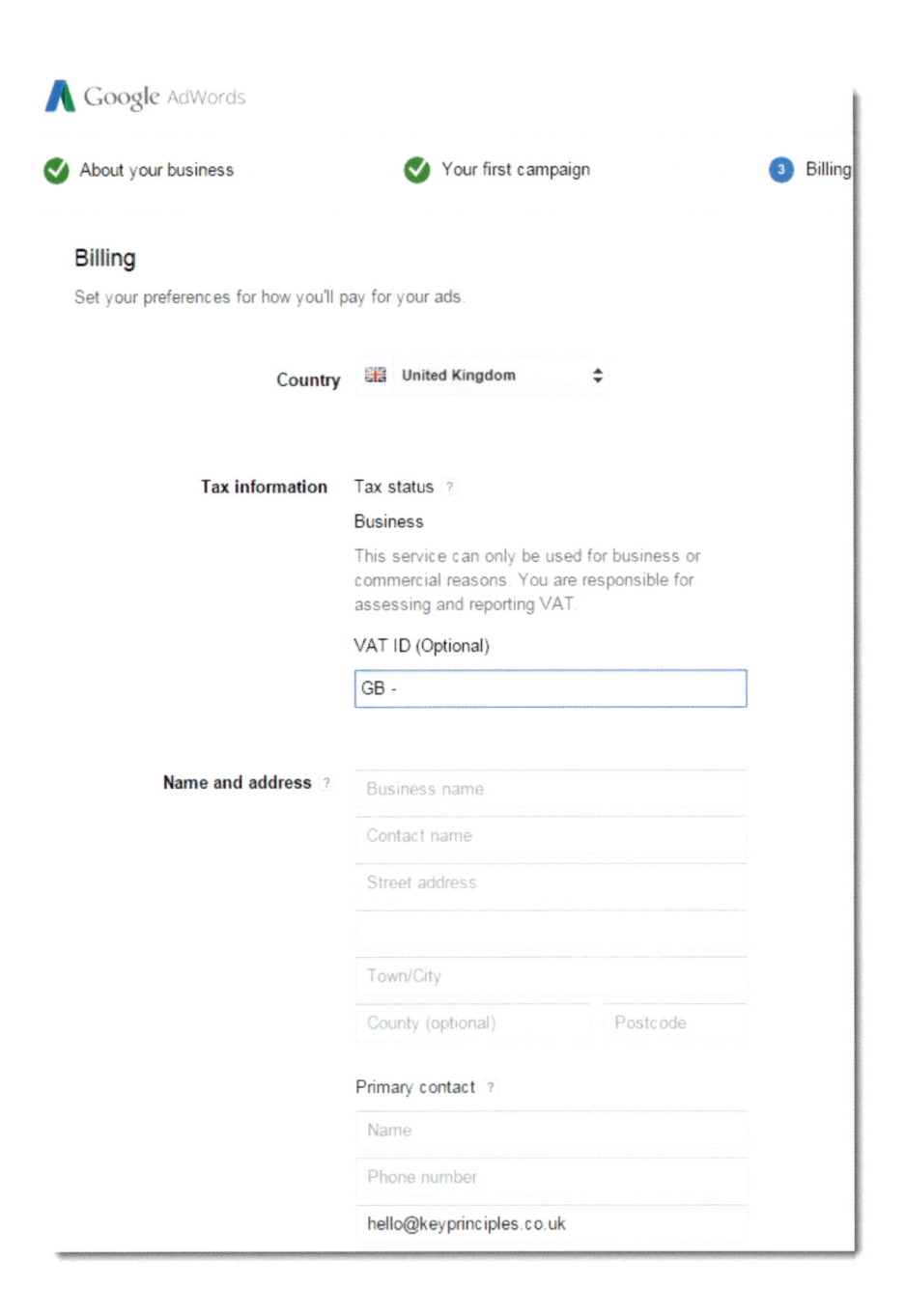

4.0 Review. You now have the chance to review the settings you have created, simply scroll down and agree to Google's Terms and Conditions and press 'Finish and create campaign' button.

You'll then come to a 'Well done!' screen where you may be asked to verify your email address. If so, go to your email inbox and click the link in the email from Google to verify your account.

You'll come to:

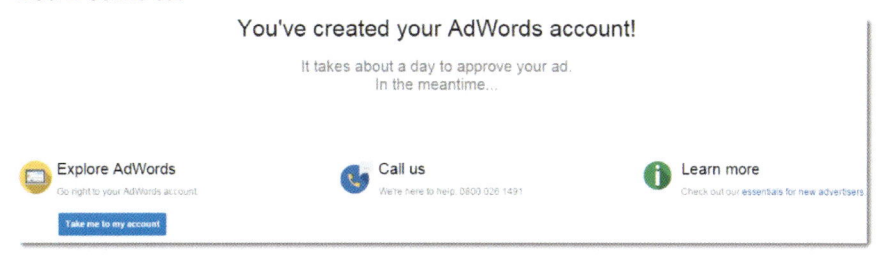

Now I'd recommend going to your account ASAP so you can pause your first campaign and Ad Group as it will currently be live and based on the few keywords you may have added with only one advert running. See the screenshot below for details of how to do this.

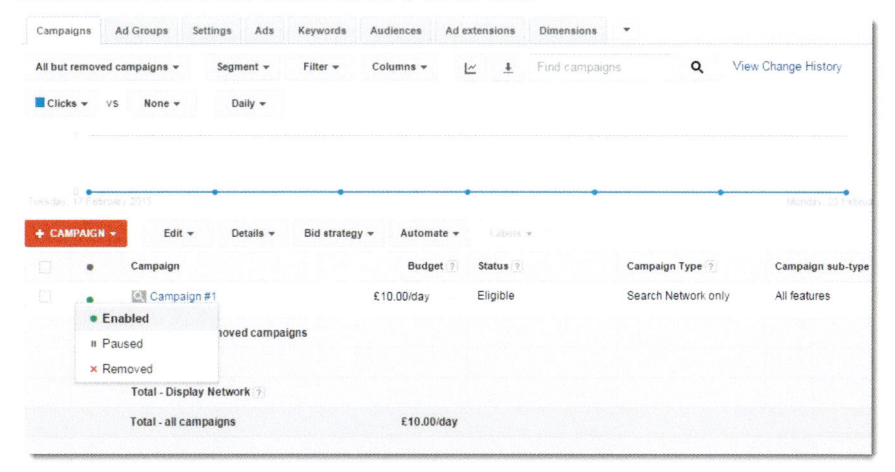

You can now review your first campaign and maybe even set up another campaign following the more detailed instructions below.

Setting Up More Campaigns

So now for actually setting up your **real** campaign… Finally, here you are, it may have taken four chapters, but you are now well and truly ready to embark on your AdWords mission. Here goes.

As you fill out all the information you need for setting up your campaign, one of the most important things to remember here is NOT to follow what Google has set as the defaults, remember they want to make money too! So make sure as you go through to check which boxes have been automatically filled in and change as appropriate.

Hopefully, from reading and implementing the actions from Chapter 3, you'll have your keyword list ready for your first campaign and may have even divided them into Ad Groups.

For the purposes of showing you how I would set up a campaign, I'm going to set up a new campaign under the new account I've set up for Key Principles. In this case I'm going to focus on Google AdWords Management and I'm going to target the East Midlands region of the UK.

1. **Preparation**
   I've already got my spreadsheet of keywords by Match Type (Broad Match Modified and Exact) and I've split them into Ad Groups. I followed the procedures outlined in Chapter 3 to get to this point.

As we go through the process I'll show you the screen shots as before.

2. **Add a new Campaign**
   So to open a new campaign simply go to the campaign tab, click the '+ CAMPAIGN' button and select the 'Search Network Only' option.

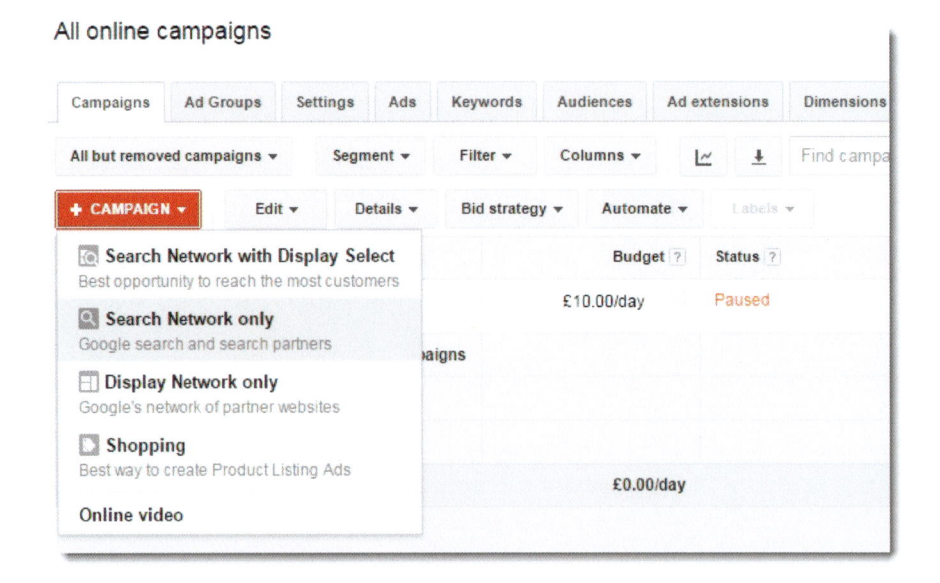

3. **Campaign Name, Type and Network**
   3.1 **Search Network Only** – Make sure '**Search Network only**' is next to 'Type'. (You might think the first thing to do is input your campaign name, but actually you should alter the settings first otherwise you'll have to input the name again at a later point.) Alter the selected options next to this button, from 'Standard' to 'All features'.
   3.2 **Campaign name** - After doing this you can now enter your campaign name, obviously this should reflect your company or detail your product or service, so for the purposes of this example we'd call it 'Google AdWords Management'. So now in the Networks section, to ensure maximum control **untick** the box labelled 'Include search partners'. This basically means your advert will not appear on sites like AOL, Ask.com and other non-Google websites.

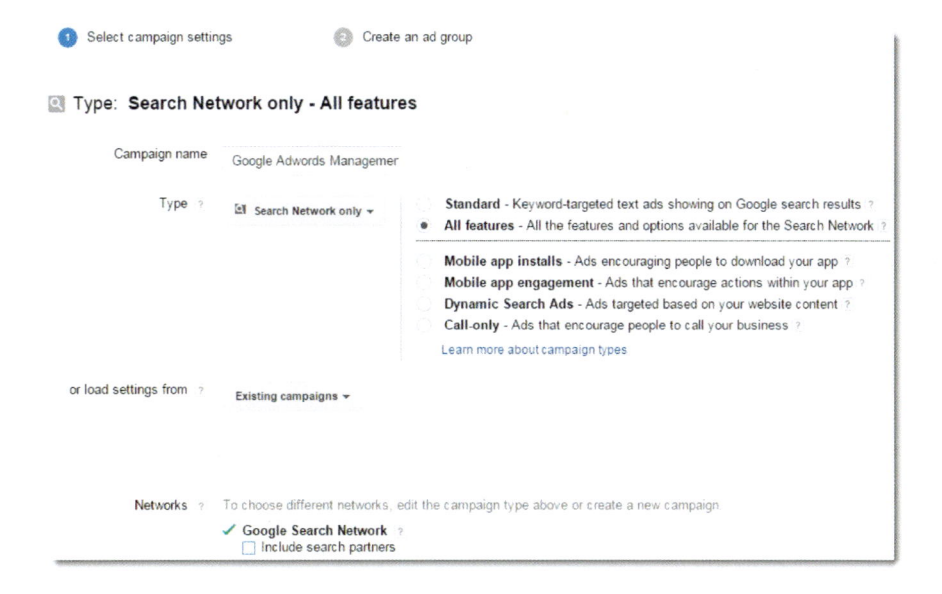

4. **Devices, Location, Language**
   4.1 **For Devices**, just leave it as it is for now. By default your ads will appear on desktops, tablets and mobiles. You can change this later if needed.
   4.2 **Location** - Okay so now the next one is Location. As a small business owner, this setting is incredibly useful for ensuring that the people who find your ad are in the right location to use your

product or service. For example, I'm an AdWords expert based in Nottingham, so I have selected the '**Let me choose**' option, and then typed 'Nottingham' into the space below, this will prevent most people searching from outside Nottingham finding my ad. I say most as for desktop searches Google uses the persons IP address unless they've let Google know where they are actually based. For the Advanced location settings, you'll see the options provided on page 43 when you click on 'Location options (advanced). Click edit next to the first option and decide how you want to target.

4.3 **Language** - Now you have the option to set the Language. Obviously if your campaign is targeting the English market, then you'll need to be using English. If your target market includes people who see English as their second language, it could be useful to use the 'All languages' option.

TIP: At a later stage, you may go back to Devices and alter the settings; if your website is mobile friendly then it's worth targeting all devices. However if you want to exclude mobiles you can specify this at a later point using the bid adjustment facility in AdWords.

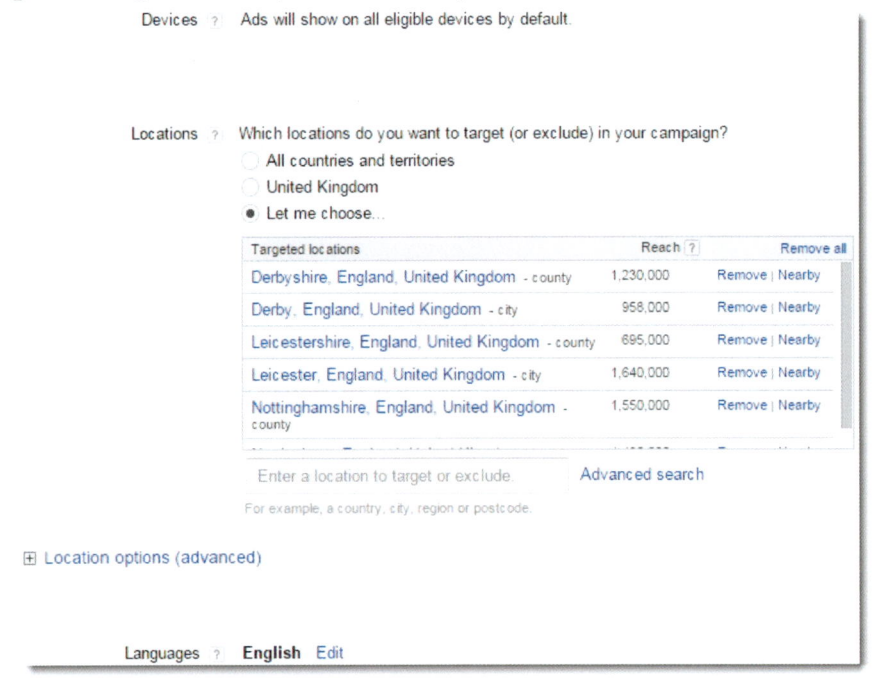

Devices	?	Ads will show on all eligible devices by default.

Locations	?	Which locations do you want to target (or exclude) in your campaign?
		○ All countries and territories
		○ United Kingdom
		● Let me choose...

Targeted locations	Reach ?	Remove all
Derbyshire, England, United Kingdom - county	1,230,000	Remove | Nearby
Derby, England, United Kingdom - city	958,000	Remove | Nearby
Leicestershire, England, United Kingdom - county	695,000	Remove | Nearby
Leicester, England, United Kingdom - city	1,640,000	Remove | Nearby
Nottinghamshire, England, United Kingdom - county	1,550,000	Remove | Nearby

Enter a location to target or exclude.   Advanced search
For example, a country, city, region or postcode.

⊞ Location options (advanced)

Languages	?	**English** Edit

The cities and counties are shown below with the Location options (advanced) opened by clicking on it.

```
Locations  ?   Targeted locations:
                 • Derby, England, United Kingdom (city)
                 • Leicester, England, United Kingdom (city)
                 • Nottingham, England, United Kingdom (city)
                 • Derbyshire, England, United Kingdom (county)
                 • Leicestershire, England, United Kingdom (county)
                 • Nottinghamshire, England, United Kingdom
                   (county)
               Edit    View location info »

⊟ Location options (advanced)

         Target  ?   People in, searching for or who show interest in my targeted location   Edit

         Exclude ?   People in, searching for or who show interest in my excluded location   Edit
```

For maximum control you may wish to change the Target to 'People in my targeted location', although the other options are fine too.

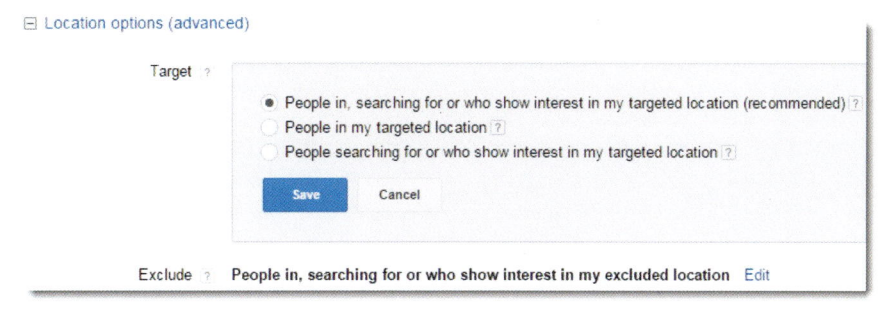

```
⊟ Location options (advanced)

         Target  ?
                   ● People in, searching for or who show interest in my targeted location (recommended) ?
                   ○ People in my targeted location ?
                   ○ People searching for or who show interest in my targeted location ?
                   [ Save ]   Cancel

         Exclude ?   People in, searching for or who show interest in my excluded location   Edit
```

5. **Bid Strategy**

   Bid Strategy is where most small business owners set their bids too low out of fear of losing money and in fact end up preventing their campaigns from reaching their potential. The amount you'll have to bid varies from sector to sector depending on how competitive the market is and how well you've set up your campaign. So before you set your bids there are two things you need to remember:
   1) LIFETIME VALUE OF THE CUSTOMER – like I've said before, once you get the customer hooked you'll start to reap the rewards, but you'll need to give a little for this to happen.
   2) YOU CAN EDIT THESE SETTINGS – if you do decide you've bid too high or too low, then you can go back and change it later, so don't worry.

   5.1 **Basic options** - Okay so onto editing the settings, I actually agree with Google here, so leave it as '**I will manually set my bids**' as this gives you the most control as a newcomer to AdWords.

5.2 **Default bid** - Now set your 'Default bid'. I'd recommend looking at results from the Keyword Planner as they'll give you a rough indication of bid value per keyword. If you're unsure, start at around **51p**, this can be changed later depending on your results.

5.3 **Budget** - As for Budget, I'd generally recommend starting between around £**10 and** £**20 per day** - this is enough to get your campaign off the ground, but not so much that any mistakes will be too costly. I've based my bids below on the amount suggested by Keyword Planner, which as my keywords are very competitive, are more expensive.

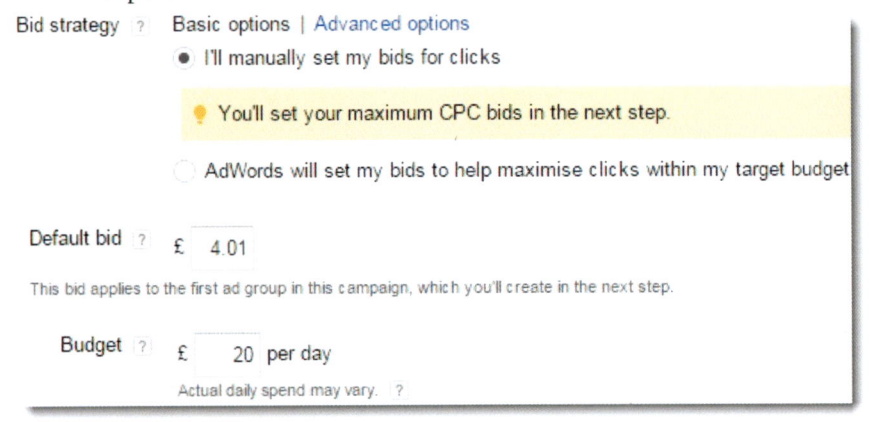

Bid strategy ?   Basic options | Advanced options
● I'll manually set my bids for clicks
💡 You'll set your maximum CPC bids in the next step.
○ AdWords will set my bids to help maximise clicks within my target budget

Default bid ? £ 4.01
This bid applies to the first ad group in this campaign, which you'll create in the next step.

Budget ? £ 20 per day
Actual daily spend may vary. ?

6. **Final Bits and Pieces**

6.1 '**Delivery method**' - The options you can see are 'Standard' or 'Accelerated Delivery'. For those starting out you can leave it as 'Standard' but if you really want to go for it, change it to 'Accelerated' to identify if you have a big enough budget.

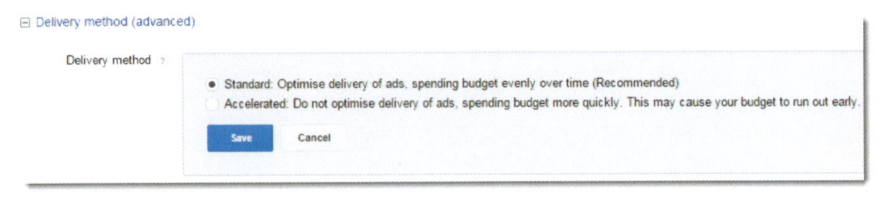

⊟ Delivery method (advanced)
Delivery method ?
● Standard: Optimise delivery of ads, spending budget evenly over time (Recommended)
○ Accelerated: Do not optimise delivery of ads, spending budget more quickly. This may cause your budget to run out early.
Save   Cancel

6.2 **Ignore the 'Ad extensions'** for the time being - we'll come back to that when we refine your campaign in the next chapter.

6.3 **Schedule settings** - you can also leave this for now, but if you want you can turn off your Ads at weekends if your service or product isn't available, or limit their showing during the evenings and overnight. To do this click the 'View ad schedule >>'

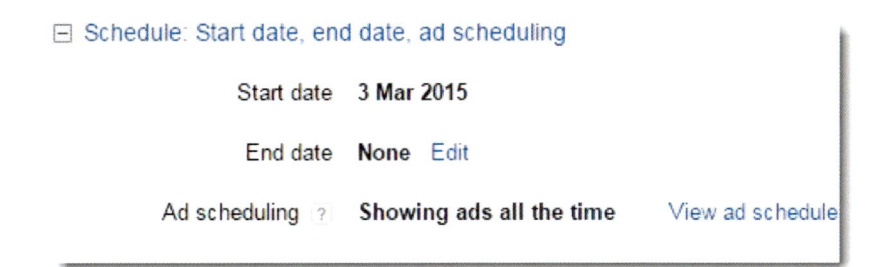

⊟ Schedule: Start date, end date, ad scheduling

         Start date   **3 Mar 2015**

         End date   **None** Edit

   Ad scheduling ?   **Showing ads all the time**   View ad schedule

And you can adjust your Schedule by clicking on the '+AD SCHEDULE' red button.

You'll come to a screen that you can easily edit and is shown below.

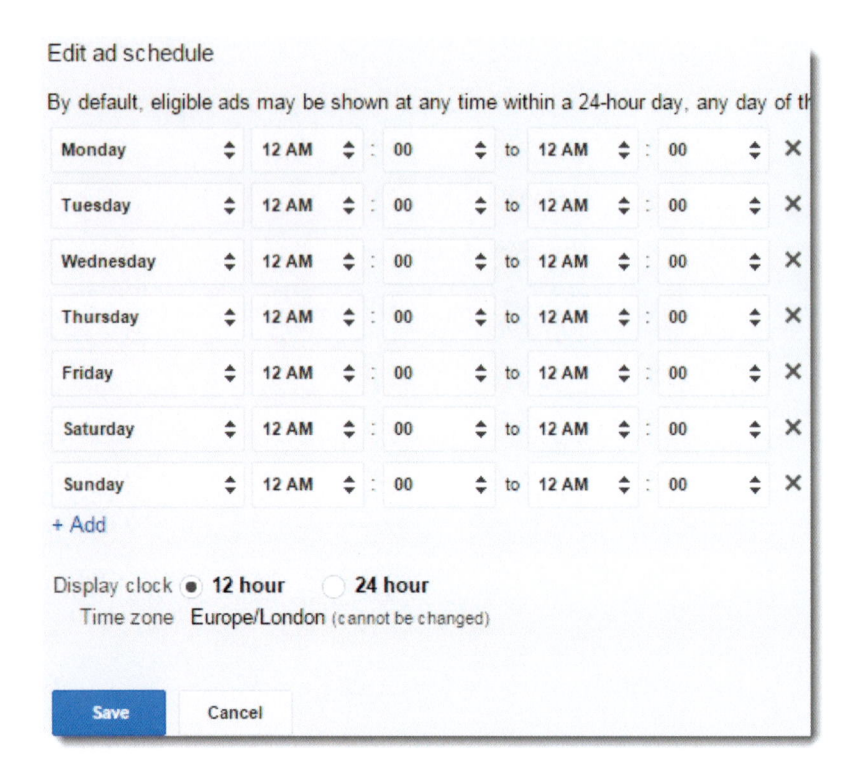

6.4 **Ad delivery** - Here you have a number of options. So that you can split text your ads effectively, I recommend the last option '**Rotate indefinitely**'. At a later date, once you are happy with your click through rates, you may want to 'Optimise for clicks'.

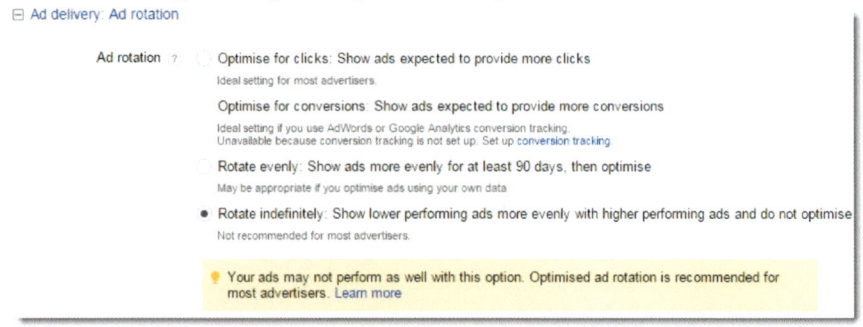

Now save and continue.

Creating Your Ad Group and Ad

Google will now have taken you along to the next step - creating your Ad Group. The name of your Ad Group needs to reflect the keywords that you will enter further down the page, so mine is simply 'AdWords Management'.

Now you are finally on to building your advert. As you will be able to see, the layout of the advert is simple enough:
- Headline
- Description line 1
- Description line 2
- Display URL
- Landing Page

There are a maximum number of characters for each line, so you'll have to bear that in mind when writing your ad.

- The **Headline** - needs to reflect the product or service you are selling, but more importantly, it needs to include one of the keywords in your Ad Group to increase the chances of your ad being displayed and clicked on.

    The **Description Lines** - both need to feature powerful verbs, calls to action, prices and offers. Calls to action like 'Buy now', 'Order here' etc. will catch the eye of the searcher, while prices and offers give them an indication of what you're offering. More specifically, line 1 should explain the details of your product/ service, whilst line 2 should describe a feature or offer, which could be financial information, to really hook in the searcher.

- The **Display URL** – this is the link which will be displayed in your advert, which people may remember, so a link containing one of the keywords in your Ad Group would be perfect for this – this would also show up in bold on the advert if the searcher included the keyword in their search query. You have to include your website URL and then you can add a keyword. See the example below www.keyprinciples.co.uk/Adwords.

- The **Landing Page** – this needs to be the most relevant website page for the campaign or Ad Group. If the searcher is looking for a specific product or service which you sell, take them directly to that page of your website. Most searchers are quite lazy; if they have to trawl through your site looking for the right page, chances are, they'll just click back and find another ad that gives them what they want straight away. So select the recommended **'Final URL'** and enter an actual web address below. Landing pages are very important for making the right first impression, so make sure yours is good and consider creating specific landing pages.

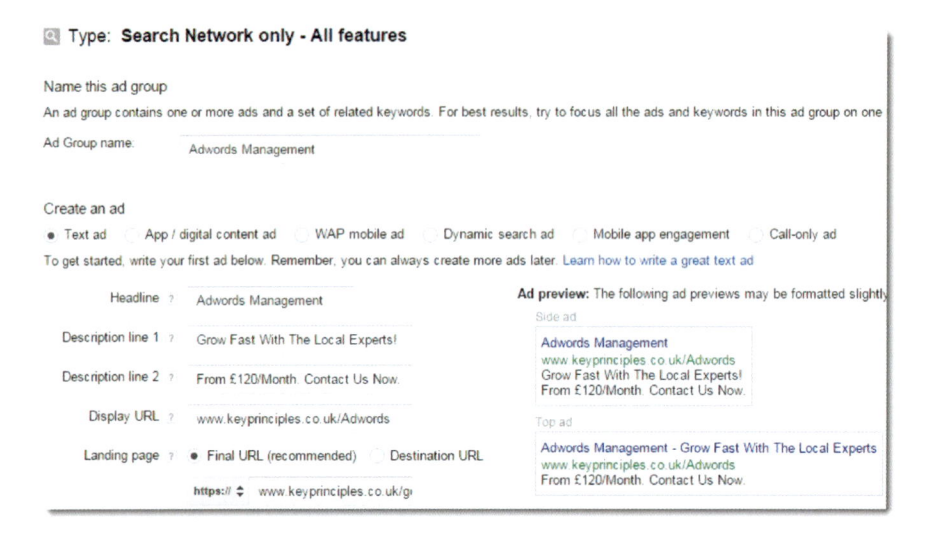

Before your ad is complete, you need to input those all-important keywords and potentially set your default bid. So type, or copy and paste, your keywords into the box provided, including all the variations of Broad Match Modified and Exact (if you are using Exact). Then leave your default bid as it is – it will be the same figure as you indicated when setting up your campaign.

So now 'Save and continue', you have your very first campaign and Ad Group set up, congratulations!

Keywords

⊟ Select keywords
Your ad can show on Google when people search for things related to your keywords.

Tips
- Start with 10-20 keywords.
- Be specific: avoid one-word keywords. Choose phrases that customers would use to search for your products and services.
- By default, keywords are broad-matched to searches to help you capture a wider range of relevant traffic. Use match types to control this.
- Learn more about choosing effective keywords.

Enter one keyword per line.

No sample keywords available.

```
+Adwords +Campaign +Management
+Adwords +Management
+Adword +Campaign +Management
+Adwords +Manager
+Adwords +Campaign +Manager
+Adword +Management
+Adwords +Bid +Management
+Campaign +Management +Adwords
+Adwords +Account +Manager
+Adwords +Account +Management
+Manage +Adwords +Campaign
+Adwords +Management
+Adwords +Managers
+Adword +Manager
[Adwords Campaign Management]
[Adwords Management]
[Adword Campaign Management]
[Adwords Manager]
[Adwords Campaign Manager]
[Adword Management]
```

Estimate search traffic

Important note: We cannot guarantee that these keywords will improve your campaign performance. We reserve the right to disap

Maximum cost per click (Max. CPC)

You can influence your ad's position by setting its maximum cost-per-click (CPC) bid. This bid is the highest price you're

Default bid ? £ 4.01
You can set keyword-level bids separately.

Adding Your Negatives

However whatever you do, don't sit back and think your campaign and Ad Group is complete, IT'S NOT. You must remember to now go and add your **Negative keywords**! To do this click onto your keywords tab, scroll past all your keywords to the bottom of the page where you'll see the option to add **Negative keywords**. How sneaky are Google to hide away where the Negative keywords need to be input? And how easy it could be to forget to add them!

So to confirm, click onto your keywords tab:

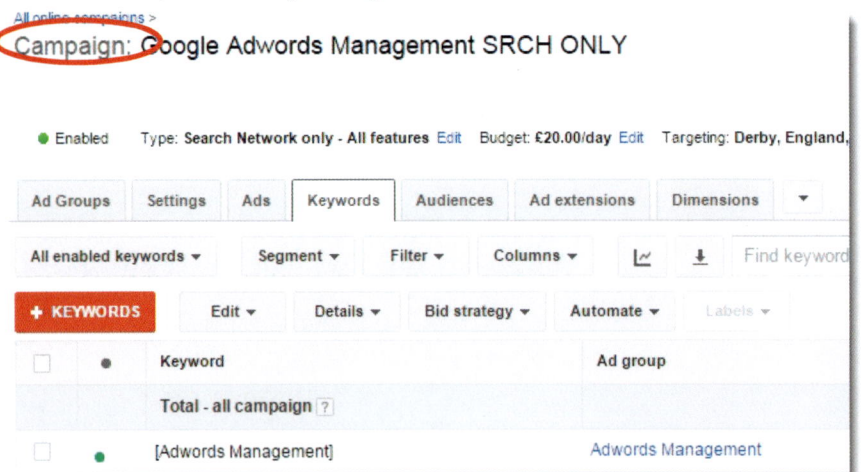

Scroll all the way down to the bottom of your keywords and you'll see Negative keywords:

| | | +Adwords +Management +Service | Adwords Management Service |
| | | +Google +Adwords +Management +Service | Adwords Management Service |

Total - all enabled keywords ?

Total - search ?

Total - Display Network ?

Total - all campaign ?

⊞ Negative keywords ?

Click on 'Negative keywords' and you'll then be given the option to add in Negative keywords at either the Ad Group or campaign level. I suggest doing it at the campaign level at the moment. So select add keywords and type or copy and paste in the words or phrases that you do not want to appear for.

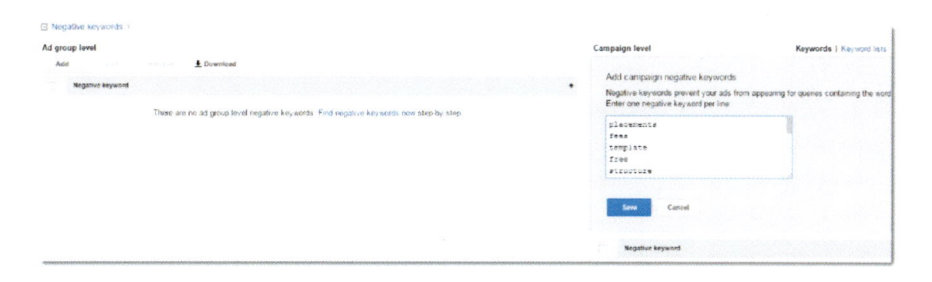

Eat, sleep, **SPLIT TEST**, REPEAT

You have just set up the very basics, and over the course of this book I'll go through all the ways you can improve your campaigns and adverts. The very first thing you can do to begin this process is to **Split Test** your ads.

Split testing is really important. You can run two ads alongside each other and see which is performing the best in terms of click through rate and conversion rates. You can overtime improve how well your adverts perform. Create the second ad exactly the same way you did previously but alter it. Include the same headline, but you could include a different message, so perhaps change the content of Description line 1 or 2, or both.

Once you have spotted which ad is performing best, pause the lower performing one and create another to split test again. ALWAYS HAVE TWO ADS UP AND RUNNING. You can repeat this process time and time again, each time trying to beat the best performing advert.

As you can see from the image below, I have set up four different ads; two for desktops and two for mobiles. I will see which performs the best and then try to beat the best performing one.

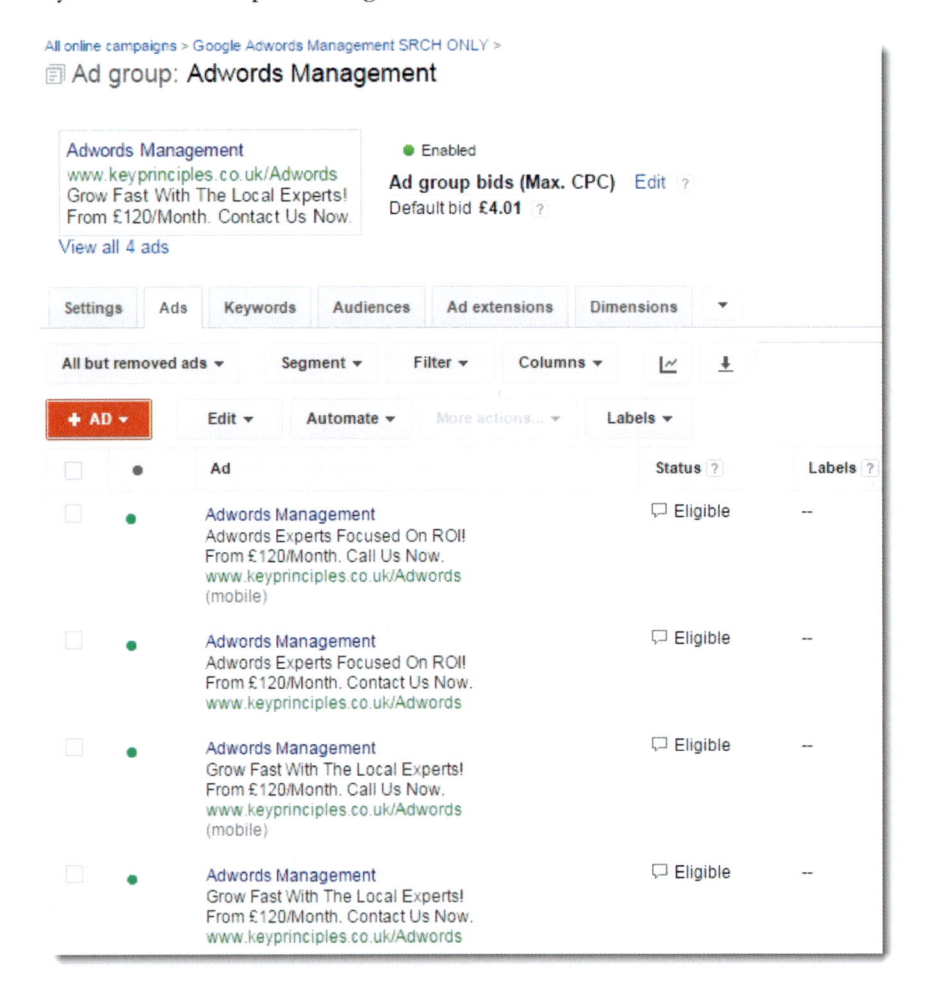

All online campaigns > Google Adwords Management SRCH ONLY >
Ad group: **Adwords Management**

Adwords Management	
www.keyprinciples.co.uk/Adwords	● Enabled
Grow Fast With The Local Experts!	Ad group bids (Max. CPC) Edit ?
From £120/Month. Contact Us Now.	Default bid £4.01 ?

View all 4 ads

Settings | **Ads** | Keywords | Audiences | Ad extensions | Dimensions

All but removed ads ▼ | Segment ▼ | Filter ▼ | Columns ▼

+ AD ▼ | Edit ▼ | Automate ▼ | More actions... ▼ | Labels ▼

	Ad	Status ?	Labels ?
●	Adwords Management Adwords Experts Focused On ROI! From £120/Month. Call Us Now. www.keyprinciples.co.uk/Adwords (mobile)	Eligible	--
●	Adwords Management Adwords Experts Focused On ROI! From £120/Month. Contact Us Now. www.keyprinciples.co.uk/Adwords	Eligible	--
●	Adwords Management Grow Fast With The Local Experts! From £120/Month. Call Us Now. www.keyprinciples.co.uk/Adwords (mobile)	Eligible	--
●	Adwords Management Grow Fast With The Local Experts! From £120/Month. Contact Us Now. www.keyprinciples.co.uk/Adwords	Eligible	--

So there you have it; a campaign and at least two ads. The next few chapters will look at refining your campaign and individual ads to maximise their potential; all with the aim of saving you money and increasing the leads and sales generated for your business.

TIP: All the way along Google provides a little '?' icon. If you hover over the '?', Google gives you a handy explanation of the term.

Rapid Recap

- The structure of AdWords is simple enough to understand; first you have your account, within which are your campaigns, which in turn hold your Ad Groups each with their individual set of keywords and ads.
- Google have broken down the setting up of your first account into four stages, these are:
    - About your business
    - Your first campaign
    - Billing
    - Review

    You shouldn't worry too much about the settings you put into place whilst creating your first campaign, as you can always go back and edit these settings or pause the initial campaign entirely if you wish.
- Whether you are happy with the campaign you have created or not, at some point you are going to want to create another one, so Google has again broken down this process into 4 areas which you will need to think about. These are:
    - Campaign Name, Type and Network
    - Devices, Location and Language
    - Bid Strategy
    - Final Bits and Pieces (my name for it, not Google's!)
- You must remember the key to success in Google AdWords is constant improvement, so it is important to never be idle and simply let your ads just run. Always split test your adverts so that you can keep improving your campaigns.

Below I have written a 'Chapter Checklist' which is a very, very basic version of the above instructions so if you ever just need a quick reminder as you're creating a new campaign you can have a skim over the following and hopefully it will provide a useful prompt and checklist!

Chapter Checklist
Creating Your Campaign:
Campaign Name, Type and Network
- ✓ Change to 'Search network'.
- ✓ Tick box for 'All features'.
- ✓ Enter campaign name.
- ✓ Untick 'Include search partners'.

Devices, Location and Language
- ✓ Leave 'Devices' as it is.
- ✓ Select 'Let me choose' and type in location/s.
- ✓ Under Location options (Advanced) choose your preferred targeting.
- ✓ Set Language as English or All Languages or whatever is appropriate.

Bid Strategy
- ✓ Set as 'I will manually set my bids'.
- ✓ Set default bid as appropriate or at around 51p to start.
- ✓ Set budget to between £10 and £20 per day.

Final Bits and Pieces
- ✓ Leave as Standard delivery or Accelerated to really go for it!
- ✓ For Ad delivery, select option 'Rotate indefinitely'.

Creating your Ad:
- ✓ Fill in a Headline, Description lines, Display URL and Landing Page (Final URL).
- ✓ Add your keywords.
- ✓ Leave default bid as it is.
- ✓ **Add Negative keywords.**
- ✓ Create a second ad to split test against the first and mobile ads if you are targeting mobiles.

Split Test and Repeat

CHAPTER FIVE
IMPROVING YOUR AD

So now you've created your adverts, here is your chance to improve them. What you have created is a perfectly adequate ad which no doubt will bring you good leads and sales, but now it's time to get into the nitty gritty of what makes a truly great ad. What will make you stand out from the crowd and give you the best ROI (return on investment)?

<ins>Writing the Killer Advert</ins>
Key Points to Remember:

- **NO Posh Prose**. You're selling to real people just like you and me. They don't want to see the eloquence of your school English literature, no matter how fancy it is; the simpler the language the better. Obviously if your advert requires technical terminology to specify what you're selling then that needs to be included, but don't overcomplicate something which is designed to be short and snappy to catch the attention of your potential customer.

- **BE RELEVANT**. There is nothing worse than getting your advert high on Google, but suffering from unnecessary clicks which waste you money. To avoid this you must be very clear in your advert what product or service you are selling so that you attract the right customers.

- **DON'T Over Hype**. Of course you want to tempt your customer in by exciting them with your product or service and any potential offers you have, but it is very easy to go overboard. People respond to a bit of enthusiasm, but too much and it is a real turn off to any potential buyer. You need to establish a middle ground; enough hype to attract attention, but not too much to scare them off.

<ins>The Advert Breakdown</ins>
THE HEADLINE:
The headline is the star of the show in your advert. It is the first thing people

read when seeing your ad and it will most likely be what they remember, so it better be good. You have 25 characters or less to impress your potential customer and get them to click, so you need to make every character count. And those 25 characters include spaces and any punctuation!

The focus of your headline should be your keyword, seeing a keyword in your headline is the first indication to your customer that they've found what they're looking for. And your keywords will appear in **bold** if the searcher included it in their search, which certainly makes your headline attract further attention.

With this in mind, you need to remember to create Ad Groups around themes or similar phrases, or even create Ad Groups for each of your keywords, so that you fully maximise your chances of the headline being in bold text and getting clicks which lead to conversions.

Your headline doesn't need to be showy or overly exciting; it simply needs to reflect the needs of the searcher. With the research you've already done about your target audience you should know what they are looking for and so you should write your headline to reflect this.

Take my client TMS Motor Group for example. TMS is a dealer for Volvo Cars and the headline of one of their most successful ads is 'Volvo Dealers Hinckley'. It says exactly what they are and what they are offering so the chances of unwanted clicks are low and the chance of a good click through rate and conversions is high. Result!

TIP: With your headlines and the text throughout, capitalise the first letter of each word e.g. Volvo Dealers Hinckley. This technique is known to improve click through rates and the TMS advert below has a CTR above 25%!

TMS Motor Group Advert Example

Volvo Dealers Hinckley — Headline includes relevant keywords
Customers Come First At TMS Volvo. — Line 1 includes why TMS is different
View Our Volvo Range & Contact Us! — Line 2 includes clear calls to action
www.tmsmotorgroup.co.uk/VolvoDealer — Display URL includes relevant keywords

THE AD TEXT:

You've got them hooked with your headline, now to reel them in with your ad text. This time you have two lines each with a maximum of 35 characters per line, so whilst you have slightly more to play with, space is still limited so you need to be concise.

As I said in the previous chapter, each line has a different purpose, use them to their full effect and you're onto a winner. In your description lines you need to convey

- i) What your product or service is/ a **benefit** it will give
- ii) A **feature** of your product or service

Benefits and features are two very different things and it's useful to understand the difference. Benefits are more personal gain whereas features are the more physical gains which you can offer, so an example of a benefit would be a skill that your customer could gain from you, whereas a feature is a physical product such as a free PDF. To help you devise killer description lines, make lists of the benefits and then the features which you offer. There will be crossovers between the two, but this exercise will prove invaluable in making your advert sell itself.

So for me my lists would begin...

Benefits:
- Get to page one of Google in 30 minutes
- Increase conversions on Google AdWords
- Step by step ways to achieve success on Google AdWords

Features:
- Download our 'Mega Tips Cheat Sheet' for Free
- Online Course for creating a successful Google AdWords campaign
- 11 tips for success on Google AdWords

Once you have your benefits and features listed you can insert them into your advert easily. Put your benefits in Line 1 and your features in Line 2 as well as a call to action.

TIP: If you send those that click on your advert to a page with the same or similar text to your advert, with the offer clearly highlighted, the visitor is less likely to click the back button and more likely to perform the action you want them to perform.

Every Word Counts: Power Words and Calls to Action
The way you write your ad doesn't only depend on the structure, but also the individual words themselves. You have a very limited amount of space so every word counts in your quest to entice your customer.

With any kind of advertising, be it online or otherwise, calls to action form a central part of the ad. A call to action is a phrase that inspires a searcher to do something, in your case it could be to click on your ad or download something of interest to them or to buy something.

Below is a list of various calls to action which you could think about including in your ad depending on the purpose of your campaign.

- Call Us Now!
- Download Our Free Video
- Buy Online Today
- Call From Your Mobile

TIP: 'Call Us Now!' is a great call to action for your mobile adverts as is 'Call From Your Mobile'.

These powerful phrases are emotive and look to inspire some kind of action from the reader. At the back of this book I've added a much longer list of power words which you can include in your ad to really make it stand out.

TIP: If you can include some sort of punctuation at the end of description line 1, it moves the second line down and makes your advert bigger! It's good practice. See the screenshots below with no exclamation mark at the end of description line 1 and then with an exclamation mark.

Without Punctuation:

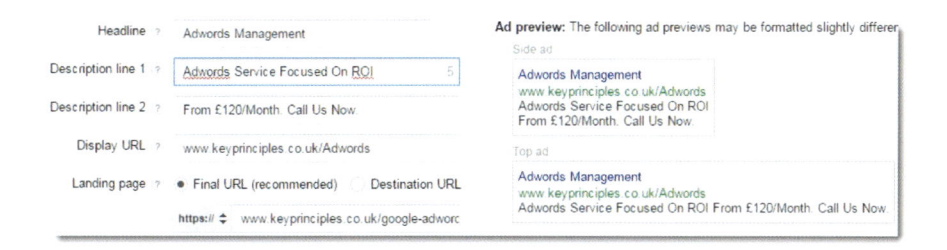

With Punctuation:

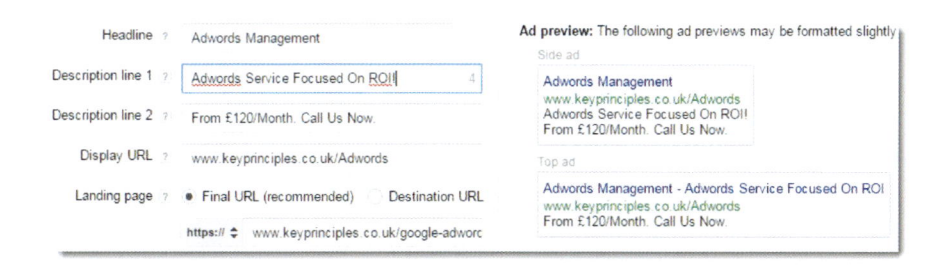

Ad Extensions

A further way of refining your ad is to create 'Ad extensions'. Ad extensions add extra information to your advert, effectively enlarging your ad. Previously I've told you to just skip over this, but now YOU'RE READY!

Many people dismiss Ad extensions as unnecessary timewasters, THIS IS A BIG MISTAKE. Think of it like this; through Ad extensions Google is giving you the opportunity to make your ads bigger. Not only does this mean they'll physically take up more room on Google, but it also boosts your

Quality Score (I'll come back to Quality Score in Chapter 8) and gives the searcher more information about the product or service you are selling which will reduce unnecessary clicks, therefore saving you money.

There are 6 different types of Ad extension which are easy enough to put in place as, you simply select the 'Ad extensions' tab on Google AdWords and choose which extension you need. As you'll be able to see in the menu on your AdWords account, the available extensions are:

- Sitelinks
- Location
- Call
- App
- Review
- Callout

Here is the list in Google:

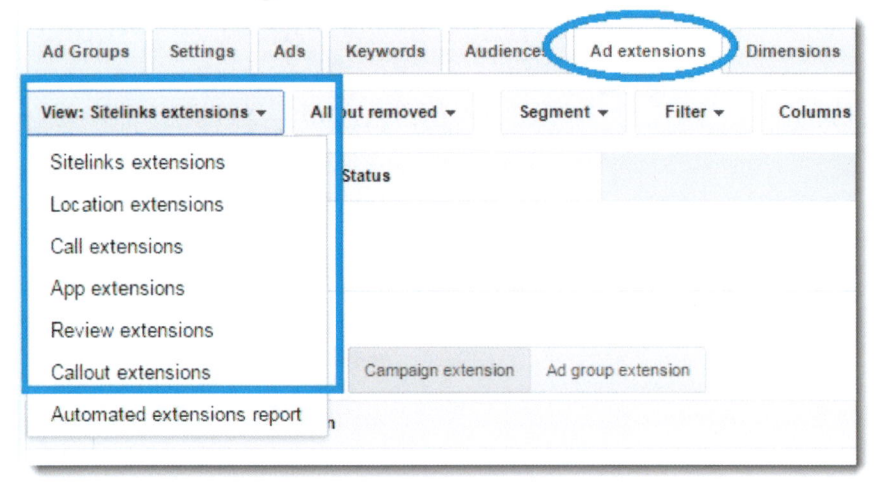

I'm only going to talk about the first three, as these are by far the most important and it is better to focus on these and get them right than to cover all 6.

Once you have filled in all the relevant information for the extensions don't expect to see them every time your ad appears on Google, as it is up to Google whether they are displayed or not. And there are several 'Terms and

Conditions' with extensions.

Terms and Conditions include:
- Number of extensions shown depends on location of your ad on the Google search results page.
- Appearance of extensions depends on the device being used – if someone is viewing your ad on a mobile it will appear differently compared to how it would on a computer.

Sitelink extensions
- ➢ Sitelinks are simply links which you can attach to your ad which will take a searcher to **different** pages on your website. This allows a potential customer to be taken straight to where they want to go, making it more likely that you will get a conversion from their click.
- ➢ Google recommends that you include at least four sitelinks which will appear just below your ad, so make the most of them.
- ➢ You can create sitelinks at the Ad Group level if you are organised and feel it's appropriate. Initially, I'd recommend you stick to doing it at a campaign level to begin with and for simplicity.
- ➢ There is also the option to add 'Enhanced Sitelinks'. With this option not only can you have extra links, but also extra lines of description under each link, which form mini ads underneath your main one. This is worth doing!
- ➢ If you are targeting mobile definitely produce mobile versions of your Sitelinks with mobile related Calls to Action in the description.
- ➢ This extension will only appear if you are within the top three on the Google search results page.

TIP: Sitelinks need to go to web pages other than the page your actual advert is going to.

Here's an example of sitelink extensions in action from a Florist based in Nottingham.

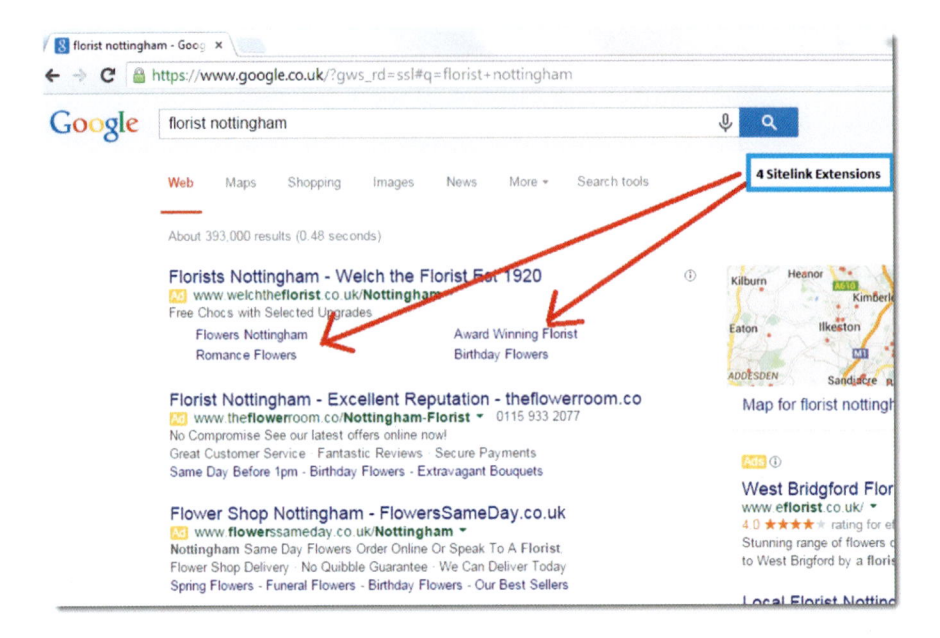

Call Extensions

➢ This extension is pretty much what is says on the tin. And is really effective when someone is searching on their mobile. They can click the link and call directly, which costs you the same as an ordinary click.

➢ Simply add your phone number to the Call Extension section.

TIP: I recommend using Google's call forwarding facility so you can monitor calls and optimise for them. This is especially important if you are not using call tracking as part of your marketing activity.

Here's the florist example again showing the actual call button.

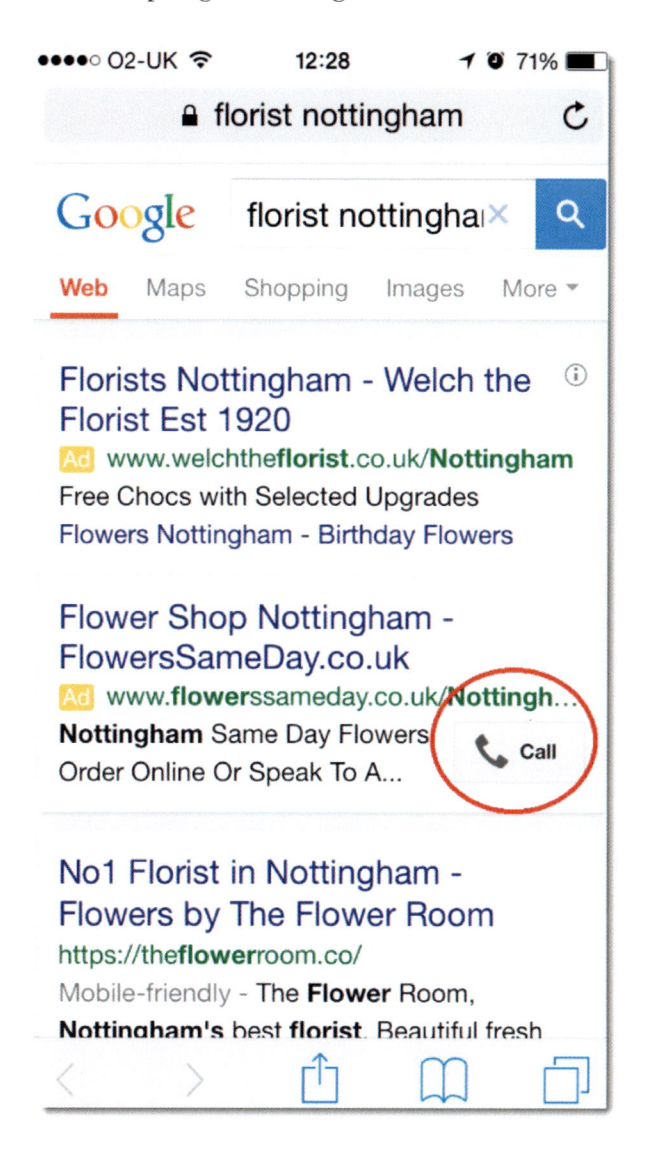

Location Extension
- ➢ This is similar to the Call Extension above, but instead shows the location of your business. As a small business owner this is ideal for you as it is unlikely your location will be well known and it is particularly important for shops, cafes and restaurants as it all happens at the location!

- Google will use your Google My Business listing – you'll need to link it. And like linking Google Analytics, this is much easier if you use the same email address for your Google My Business listing as you use for your Google AdWords account.

The Callout Extension is pretty easy to set up too if you want to look at them. They add even more text to your advert and that is never a bad thing.

Rapid Recap:

- Keep your ads simple. Use clear language with calls to action and make sure it is relevant to what you are selling and to your landing page.
- Ad text matters. Each line within your ad has a different purpose. Work on each one separately and make sure it conveys what you're selling in a clear and attractive way for your potential customer.
- Think of headlines which only attract the attention of the people who are searching for what you offer and use your keywords in your headline.
- Ad extensions are a great way of making your ads more visible on Google. Whilst there are many different types and some will only appear if you are in one of the top three positions, they make a difference and are well worth building into your campaigns.
- Keep split testing your adverts; you want to keep improving your click through rates.

Chapter Six
Landing Pages that Convert

Firstly, what is a landing page? In simple terms, the landing page is the page you are going to send searchers to when they click on your advert. Many AdWords advertisers will send their visitors to their website home page, but this is most often a mistake as the landing page needs to be more specific.

When creating an AdWords account it is easy to overlook the importance of your landing page. The landing page is essentially round two of trying to secure your customer. If it doesn't inspire the customer then all that work you've done on making your campaigns and adverts the very best they can be, will be a complete waste of time.

Research shows that you have approximately eight seconds before your visitor either chooses to stay on your site or clicks that dreaded back button, so you need to make those seconds count.

The Three Golden Rules

There are three main things which a top landing page needs to have in order to maintain the searchers interest and prevent them from returning to Google and wasting a click.

1) **RELEVANCE.** Just like every other area of your AdWords campaign, your landing page needs to be relevant. If your ad is displaying one thing and your landing page is displaying another, the chances of the searcher clicking the back button are very high indeed.

Ways to increase relevancy:
- Before you get started ask yourself these key questions; what is the goal of your landing page, i.e. do you want them to enquire further about your product or simply sign up for a free download? Who are you competing against? Who is your audience? If you work out the answer to these questions you're off to a good start.

- Reflect the headline of your ad in the landing page, or use snippets of your description lines of your ad in your headlines or on your page. This repetition of information confirms to the searcher that they have come to the right place and are just a couple of clicks away from getting what they want.
- Don't give your customer an easy way out. If you are promoting a particular product or service, make sure your landing page is focused on that product or service. Whilst you do need links to the rest of your site, don't give the searcher too many options to click onto other links as you risk distracting them from what they want. Don't have too many calls to action. Channel them where you want them to go for those vital leads and sales.

NOTE: Many first timers on AdWords use their website home page as their landing page; it is very unlikely that your home page will be the best landing page, so I'd definitely recommend using another page on your website – the most relevant page.

2) **EASY TO USE**. The truth of the matter is; human beings are lazy. When searching online people do not want to be bombarded with information, nor do they want to have to search every inch of your website to find what they are looking for. Also there is no use having a page packed full of information related to your ad if it is laid out in a way which will likely confuse your potential customer. The layout of your landing page needs to be clear, with the necessary amount of information. It needs to be easy to understand and provide the visitor with a clear call to action.

Ways to make your site easy to use:
- A **clear layout** is vital to the success of your landing page and therefore your AdWords campaign. Your information needs to be clearly spaced, with obvious breaks in the text and headings. Like I said, people are lazy, but with a well-designed format the person viewing your page can easily skim read what you have to offer.
- The **formatting** of your landing page should come across as professional. Use an appropriate font at size 12 or 14.

- As for your **colour** scheme, studies suggest that people are more receptive to information written in black on a white background, but again that depends on the style of your business. For the use of other colours consider the obvious connotations each colour provokes – yellow; happy, blue; sad etc. So if you're a company who specialises in children's parties, black and grey probably isn't your best option. And some colours simply don't work as well online.
- Use **interesting graphics** and images on your page. Visual clues such as arrows are also really good at directing your potential customer where you want them to go.
- Use **language** appropriate for what you are selling, but don't use terminology which may confuse the average searcher.
- **Calls to action** are essential for a good landing page so make sure you use them and that they stand out.
- **Make it easy for your visitor to buy** your product or get more information, so have a specific button which they can press to get what they want. You can also have a button with the option for the visitor to 'share' their findings.
- Your landing pages should not only be easy to read and understand, but also be easy on the eye. If it looks well thought out and professional, people are more likely to trust you and what you are offering.

3) PATIENCE. Don't harass your potential customer. It is very tempting to pounce on your visitor as soon as they arrive on your page, demanding an email address or other details - pages that do this are called 'squeeze pages'. Don't do this. Your potential customer won't like it and neither will Google. People appreciate the time to browse through what you have to offer before committing themselves to you, so just be patient and you'll have their contact details in no time. In fact Google tends to label landing pages with no or few links to other parts of the site, as a 'poor user experience', which therefore has a negative effect on the Quality Score.

Ways to go easy on your visitor and still get what you want:
- **Make it all about them.** Similarly to your ad text, the benefits of your product or service need to come first. The details of the features of what you're selling can wait. You need to focus on making an emotive case to

your potential customer as to the benefits of your offer. Are you going to make THEIR lives easier? Do you have the solution to THEIR worries? Whatever it may be that you can give them, now is the time to offer the solution.

- **Only ask for the information needed.** Funnel your potential customer in the direction you want them to go and then ask for their email. Remember, patience is a virtue.

Improving Your Landing Pages

- **Use Trust Signals.** These are basically the logos of other companies you have done business with, industry associations you or your company are members of or awards/qualifications you have. By displaying these on your landing page you send out the perfect message to your visitor; that you are trustworthy and successful. As an example of the use of trust signals, one client of mine for many years is PWR Lettings; a very successful letting agents in Nottingham. PWR is a member of various 'governing' bodies and this is promoted on their home page and other pages.

Shown in situ

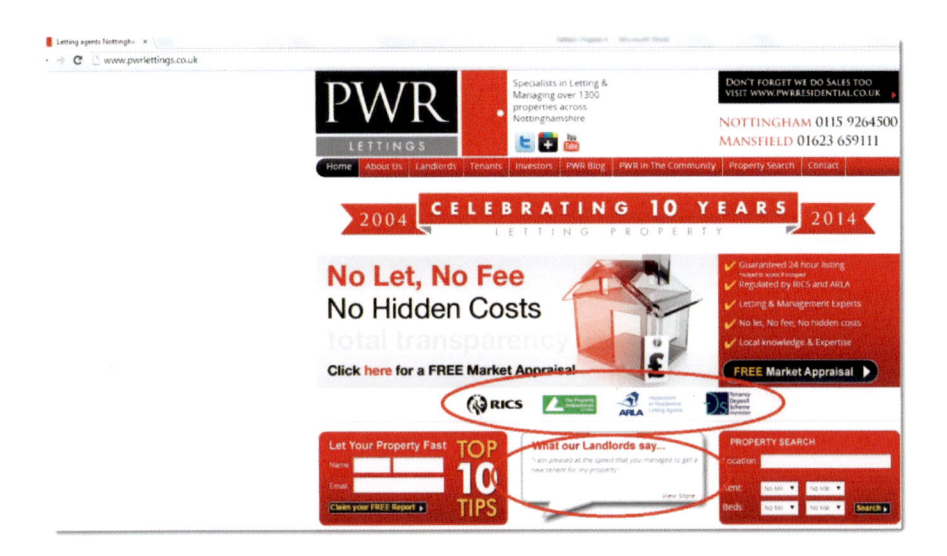

Shown larger

- **Client Testimonials.** These also work great as a further level of trust. Again PWR Lettings use testimonials effectively throughout their website. Check out the Landlord testimonials below which appear on one of their AdWords landing pages. So don't hide your testimonials away on one page, include them on various pages of your website and especially near calls to action.

Shown in situ

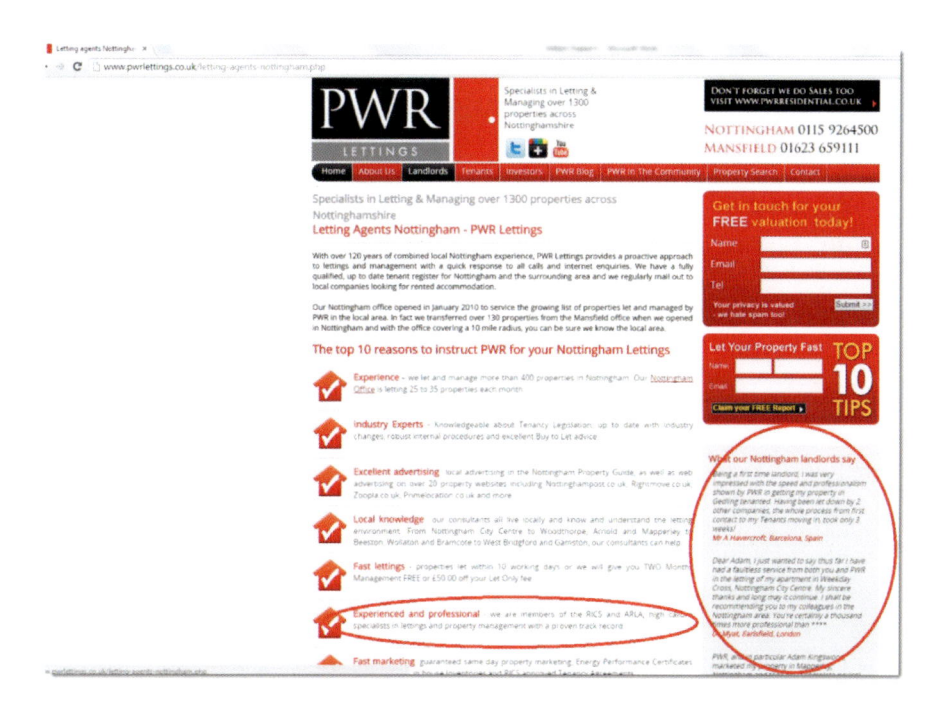

Shown larger

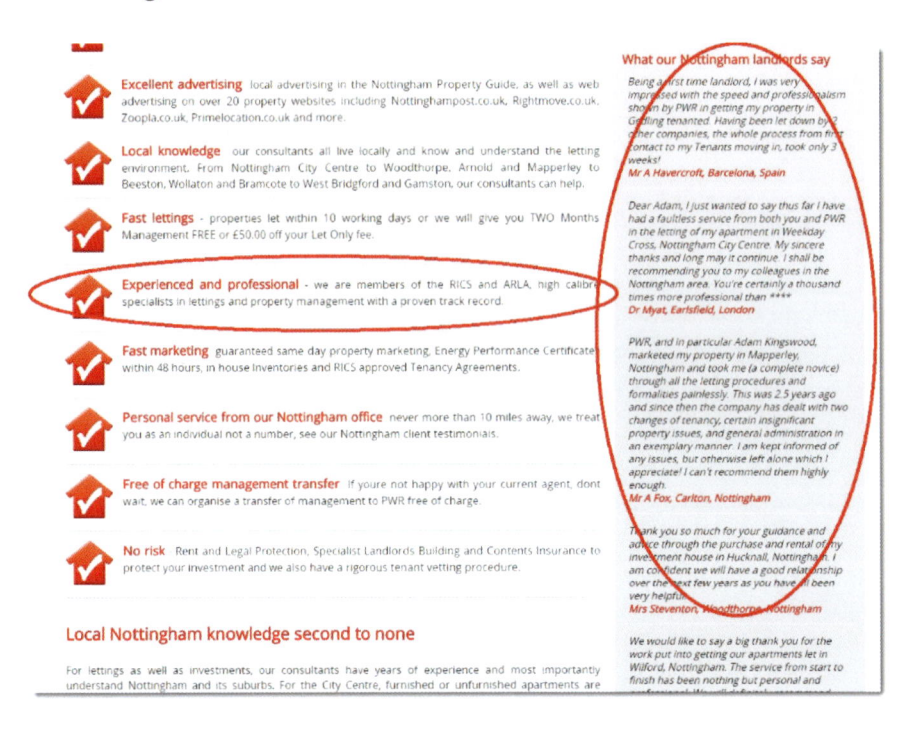

[Image of a landing page with red tick/house icons listing: Excellent advertising, Local knowledge, Fast lettings, Experienced and professional (circled in red), Fast marketing, Personal service from our Nottingham office, Free of charge management transfer, No risk. A column on the right headed "What our Nottingham landlords say" contains testimonials from Mr A Havercroft (Barcelona, Spain), Dr Myatt (Earlsfield, London), Mr A Fox (Carlton, Nottingham), and Mrs Steventon (Woodthorpe, Nottingham), circled in red. A bottom section reads "Local Nottingham knowledge second to none".]

- Finally, as with every other part of your AdWords campaign, you MUST split test your landing pages. Create different versions of your landing page and see which one performs best. This is crucial as it will impact on your conversion rates – how many visitors it takes for you to get a lead or sale.

TIP: For the greatest impact on conversion rates, don't just look at style and colours, look at what you are actually offering and the messages. Chances are you will have a much bigger affect by changing the offer than by simply changing the design of a page.

Rapid Recap:

> The success of your landing pages hinges on three factors:
>> 1) Relevancy. Make sure your landing page is relevant to your ad.
>> 2) Easy to use. This involves both language and layout, so make sure it is easy to understand and easy to navigate.

3) Patience. Don't pounce on the potential customer as soon as they click on your ad and visit your landing page. Give them time to see what you have to offer before encouraging a purchase.
- Using trust signals and client testimonials can really help potential customers trust you and what you're offering.
- SPLIT TEST. Again and again and again. The aim is to increase conversion rates; the number of enquiries or sales you receive from a given number of visitors.

Chapter Seven
Conversion Tracking

Google AdWords revolves around trying to understand what people want and giving it to them. Your campaigns, Ad Groups and adverts are all geared towards impressing potential customers and encouraging them to click on your ad and eventually become your customer. So how do you know if it's working?

The obvious questions of course include... Are you getting more leads and sales? Are they good quality leads and sales?

But with multiple campaigns, Ad Groups and adverts as well as plenty of keywords, how do you know what's working and what's not? By setting up conversion tracking, you can easily discover what's good, what's not, what's making you money, what's not, down to the very last penny.

Getting the tracking set up and working properly is so important that I generally don't work with clients unless they are prepared to get the tracking sorted before we send an AdWords campaign live. It sounds quite technical and tricky do to, but it isn't really, and if you have a good website developer they can help pop the necessary code into the right spot.

What is Conversion Tracking?
With conversion tracking you can identify which keywords, adverts and landing pages are bringing you the best return so that you can make future decisions based on facts rather than hunches.

If you want to improve your AdWords campaigns; spend less money for more leads and sales, you have to set up conversion tracking, it's that simple. By doing this, you can optimise your AdWords campaigns based on which keywords generate conversions, leads and sales, and which adverts and landing pages help to generate these leads and sales.

There are many ways of setting up conversion tracking. Below are two options; one through Google AdWords and one through Google Analytics.

Step by Step Way To Set Up Conversion Tracking Through Google AdWords

#1 FINDING CONVERSIONS ON ADWORDS

Go to the Tools tab on AdWords, click on it to reveal the drop down menu, where you will see 'Conversions'.

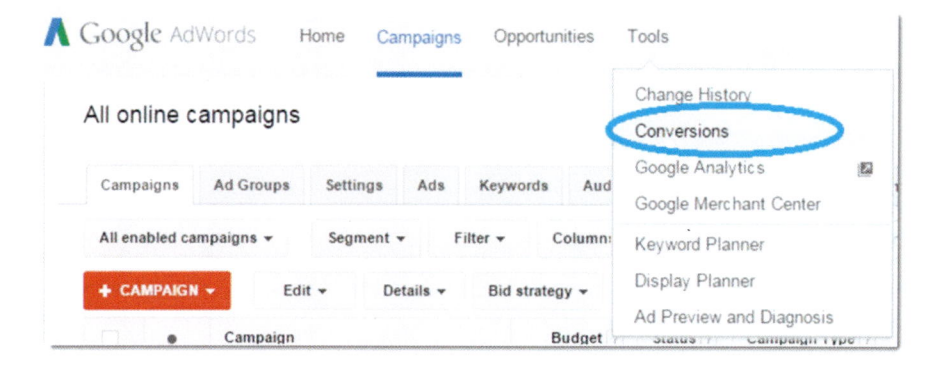

Then you come to this page and click the red icon '+CONVERSION'.

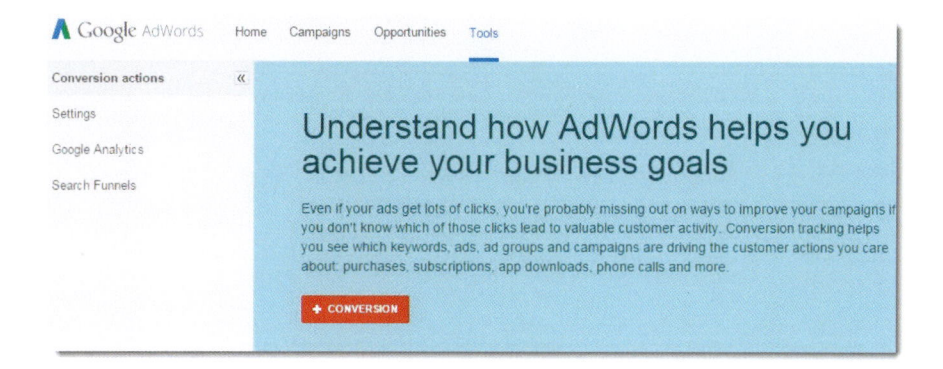

You'll be taken to the page below – **Conversion Source**.

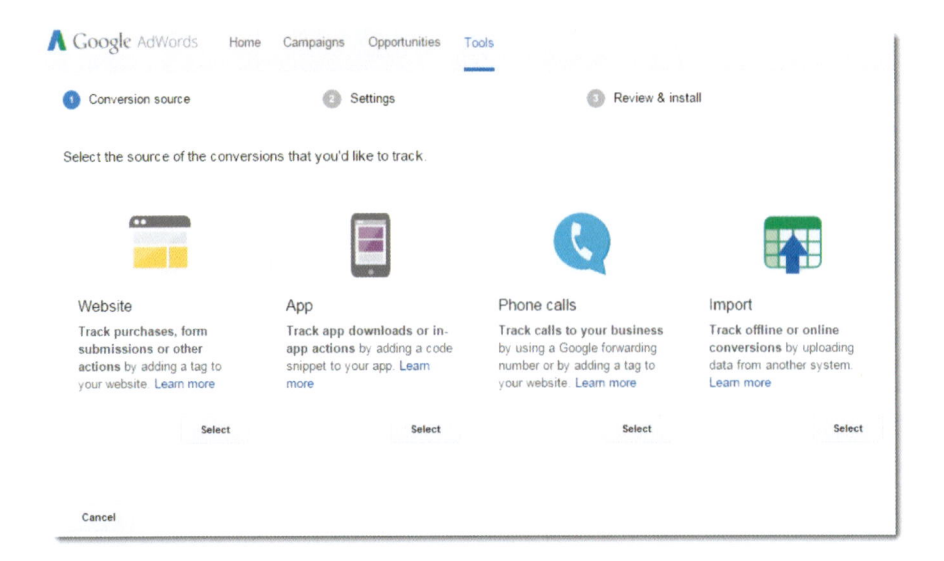

#2 CONVERSION SOURCE COMPLETED

You will need to decide what the source of the conversion is, effectively where it is coming from. In most cases this will be 'Website' or 'Phone calls' but it could be any of the options above.

For the purposes of this example I selected 'Website' and came to the following page:

NOTE: You'll need to have set up specific 'Thank you' pages to use the web page option for tracking conversions. If you can't do this, your web developer will certainly be able to help you.

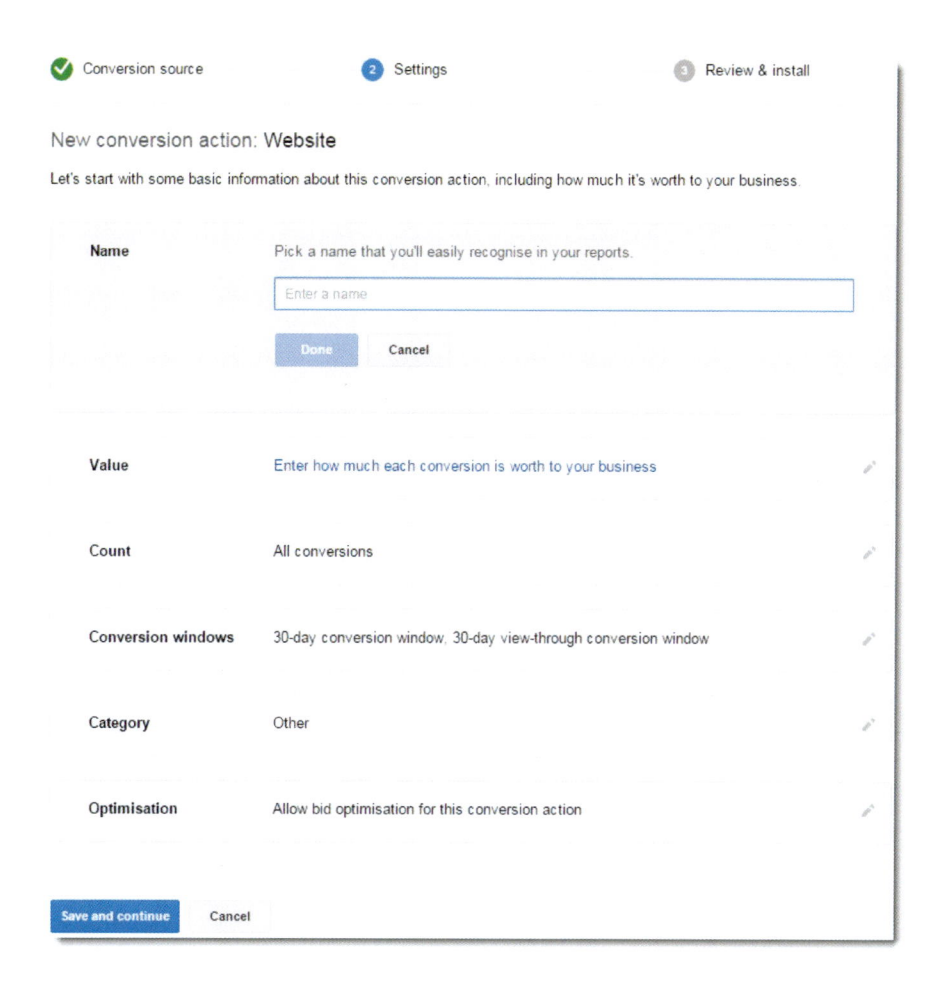

#3 CONVERSION NAME

I've added 'AdWords Service Enquiry' as this best suits the action someone has taken in this instance and I've clicked done.

#4 CONVERSION VALUE

You have three options here as shown on the screenshot.

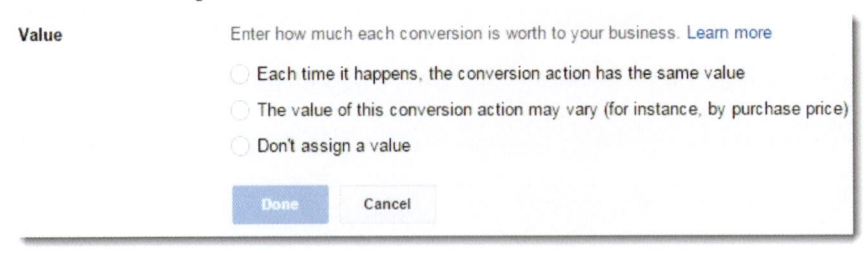

In this example, I selected 'Each time it happens, the conversion action has the same value' as I cannot identify an actual value such as purchase price at this stage.

Your conversion value is crucial in helping you to improve your account and campaigns. The easiest way to explain what your conversion value is and how it works is to equate it to a points system. Each proper conversion is worth 1 point. So that could be either a call, or a request for a quote.

However, you may not consider downloading a free PDF or signing up to a free newsletter as a full conversion. With these types of actions you could assign a nominal value of say 0.5 instead of 1. Depending on the name/purpose you have given this particular conversion, type either 0.5 or 1 into the box provided.

I have given a value of 1 GBP as I'm simply counting the conversions in this instance.

Click 'Done' and move to Count.

#5 COUNT

Here you have two options: 'Unique' or 'All'. 'Unique conversions' groups together actions made by the same person, say one person makes several purchases; that would count as one conversion. Whereas the option 'All conversions' literally does just that – records each individual action as a separate conversion.

In most cases I would recommend using 'All' and then click 'Done'.

Count	Choose how you'd like to count your conversions. Learn more
● All	Example: if one ad click leads to three purchases, that will count as three conversions.
○ Unique	Example: if one ad click leads to three purchases, that will count as one conversion.

[Done] [Cancel]

#6 CONVERSION WINDOWS

The Conversion Window is the amount of time the tracking system will follow the activities of a visitor to your site. The default setting is 30 days, so if someone clicks on your site once, your conversions tracking will watch out to see if they visit again for 30 days.

When it comes to 'Conversion Windows', you need to think about the nature of your business. How long from a website visit could it be before the actual enquiry or purchase is made? For low value items this may be a short space of time, but for higher value items and where people procrastinate about spending money or making a decision it could be longer. The options are limitless as you can even include a custom option. If in doubt, I recommend staying with 30 days.

TIP: If you have a long sales cycle, so for higher value items such as cars or for purchases that involve procrastination such as wills for example; it makes sense to make the Conversion Window longer. Think about your industry and decide based on your knowledge of the sales cycle.

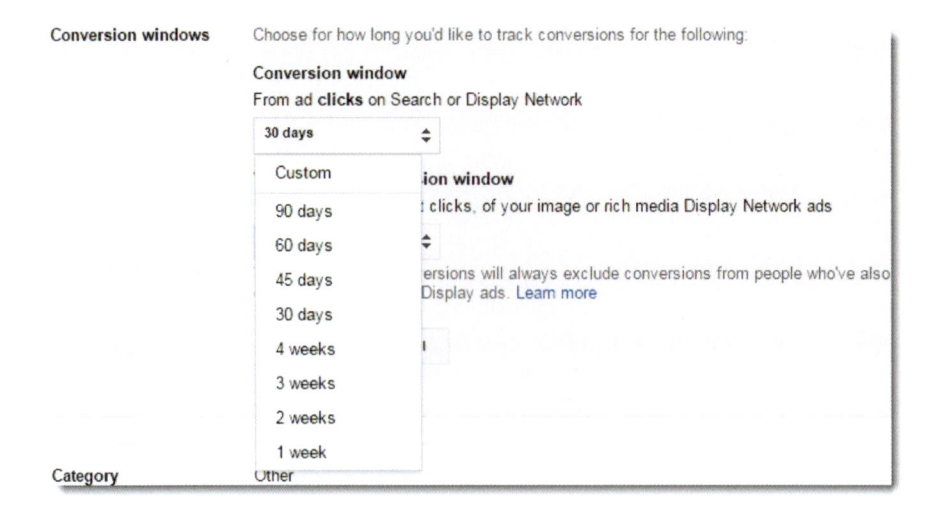

Conversion windows	Choose for how long you'd like to track conversions for the following:
	Conversion window
	From ad **clicks** on Search or Display Network

30 days	♦
Custom	ion window
90 days	clicks, of your image or rich media Display Network ads
60 days	
45 days	ersions will always exclude conversions from people who've also Display ads. Learn more
30 days	
4 weeks	
3 weeks	
2 weeks	
1 week	
Category	Other

#7 CATEGORY

As Google instructs, simply choose the category that best fits the conversion or the action the website visitor has taken. In the case of an 'AdWords Service Enquiry' it would be a lead. 'Sign up' could be for a sign up to a newsletter and 'Purchase/Sale' is where you are selling online. You also have the option of tracking when someone lands on a particular page; 'View of a key page'.

Category	Choose a category that best fits this conversion action. This will help you evaluate similar conversions in your reports.
	Other
	Purchase/Sale
	Sign up
	Lead
	View of a key page

#8 OPTIMISATION

This is a new option in the set-up and the information shown by Google is provided below.

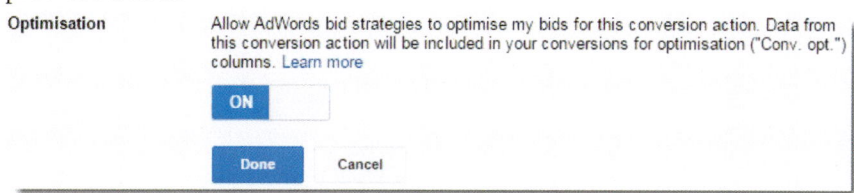

In this case, I would recommend switching off the 'Optimisation' as you want to be in control of your AdWords optimisation rather than letting Google take control.

So my final Settings look like the screen shot below:

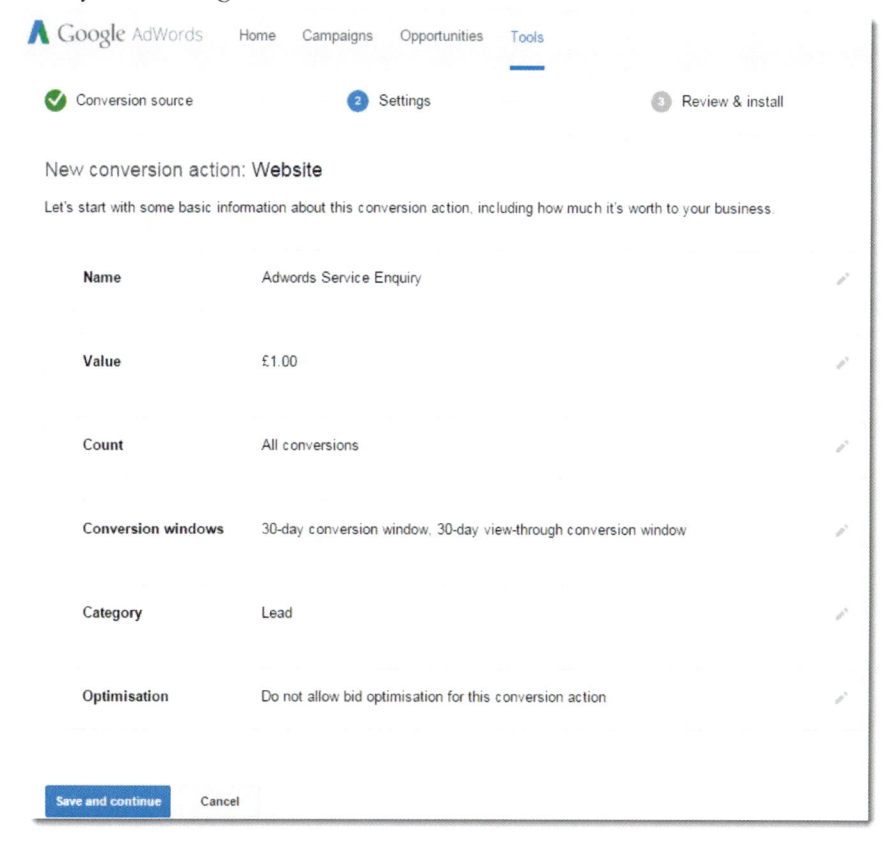

Press 'Save and continue'.

#9 REVIEW AND INSTALL

By clicking 'Save and continue' you'll come to the 'Review & install' page shown next:

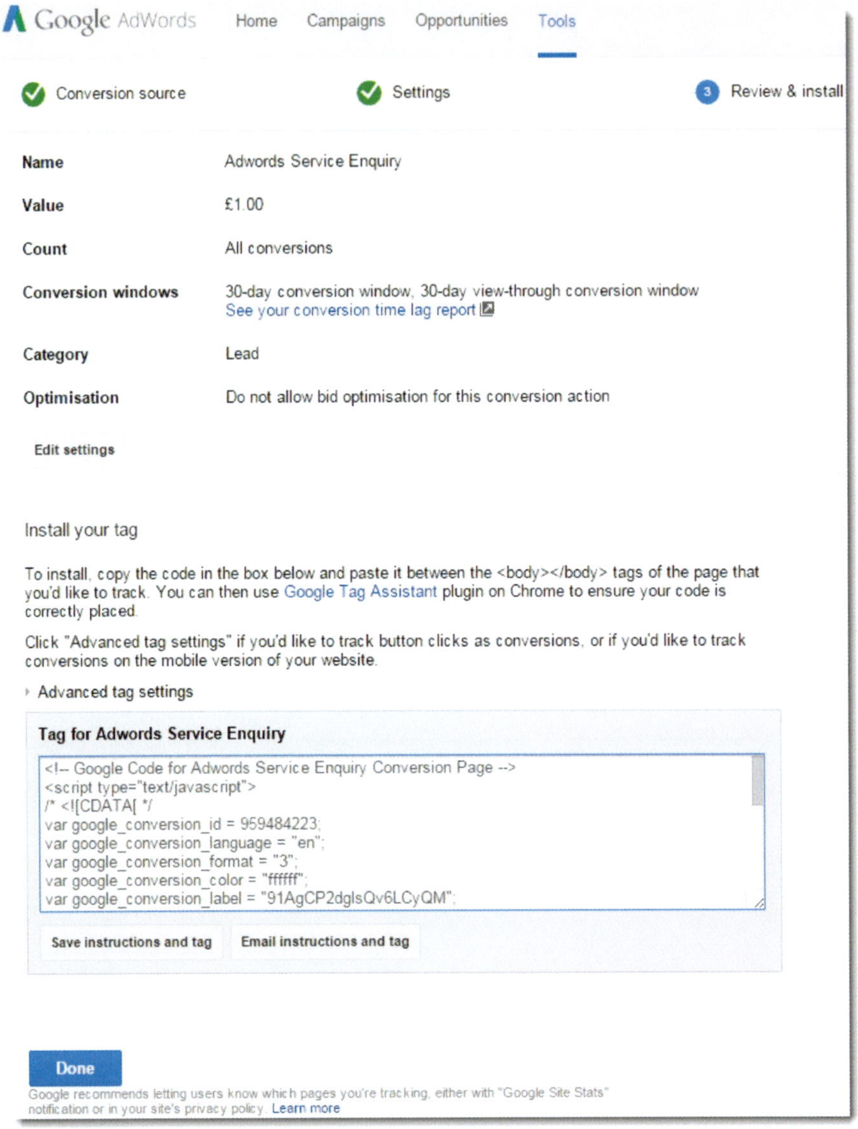
Google AdWords
Home
Campaigns
Opportunities
Tools
Conversion source
Settings
3 Review & install
Name
Adwords Service Enquiry
Value
£1.00
Count
All conversions
Conversion windows
30-day conversion window, 30-day view-through conversion window
See your conversion time lag report
Category
Lead
Optimisation
Do not allow bid optimisation for this conversion action
Edit settings
Install your tag
To install, copy the code in the box below and paste it between the <body></body> tags of the page that you'd like to track. You can then use Google Tag Assistant plugin on Chrome to ensure your code is correctly placed.
Click "Advanced tag settings" if you'd like to track button clicks as conversions, or if you'd like to track conversions on the mobile version of your website.
Advanced tag settings
Tag for Adwords Service Enquiry
<!-- Google Code for Adwords Service Enquiry Conversion Page -->
<script type="text/javascript">
/* <![CDATA[*/
var google_conversion_id = 959484223;
var google_conversion_language = "en";
var google_conversion_format = "3";
var google_conversion_color = "ffffff";
var google_conversion_label = "91AgCP2dglsQv6LCyQM";
Save instructions and tag
Email instructions and tag
Done
Google recommends letting users know which pages you're tracking, either with "Google Site Stats" notification or in your site's privacy policy. Learn more

For this part, you may want to enlist the help of your web developer.

In this instance you would add the code to the appropriate 'Thank you' page so that you can track the action. Google even tells you where on the page to put the code.

That's one done. Now you should go through your website and wherever a visitor performs an action you would like to monitor, track that action by setting up more conversions. So repeat the following steps several times, giving each a different name to allow you to track multiple aspects of your campaign.

Google Analytics and Tracking

Another way to follow your progress is through Google Analytics. This free Google tool offers much more information in comparison with AdWords Conversion Tracking. It can be useful especially if you also get visitors from natural/non-paid-for search and from other websites as it can also track any conversions they generate too.

You can set up 'Goals' in Google Analytics and as long as your Google AdWords and Google Analytics accounts are linked, you can pull through the goal information from Analytics into AdWords.

Goals are basically conversions and you can set them up in a very similar way to Conversion Tracking in Google AdWords. In fact you use 'Thank you' URLs and set up the Goals based on this. If you have Google Analytics, and I recommend you do, there is one big advantage – you don't have to mess about with more tracking code. As long as the Google Analytics tracking code is on all pages, you can simply set up the Goals and start measuring conversions.

Go to www.jackie-key.com/Goals-In-Analytics for step by step instructions on setting up Goals in Analytics.

Google is keen to encourage tracking of conversions as they want their AdWords customers to monitor closely just how effective AdWords is so they will keep using it.

There are in fact various other options for tracking what's happening including ecommerce tracking and Google Tag Manager. For a simple quick start, I'd suggest using the Conversion Tracking in AdWords or Google

Analytics with Goals. As you start to see the results, it is important to make sure you improve your tracking and Google Tag Manager can certainly help by tracking much more.

Adding Conversion Columns at All Levels

Once you have set up your conversions, you'll be able to add new columns to your account at all levels including campaign, Ad Group and keyword level.

Simply go to 'Columns', 'Customise Columns' as shown:

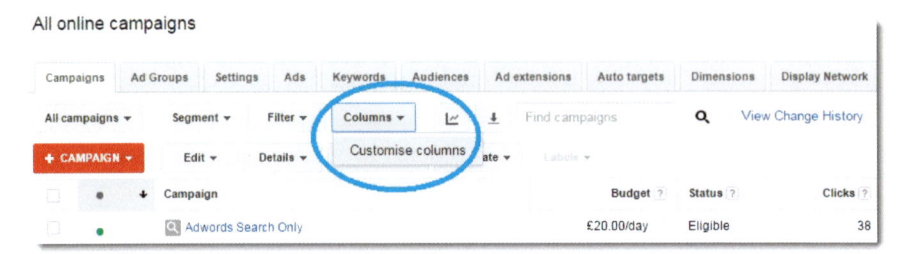

You'll come to the screen below. Click 'Conversions' and simply add the metrics you want to follow and click 'Apply'.

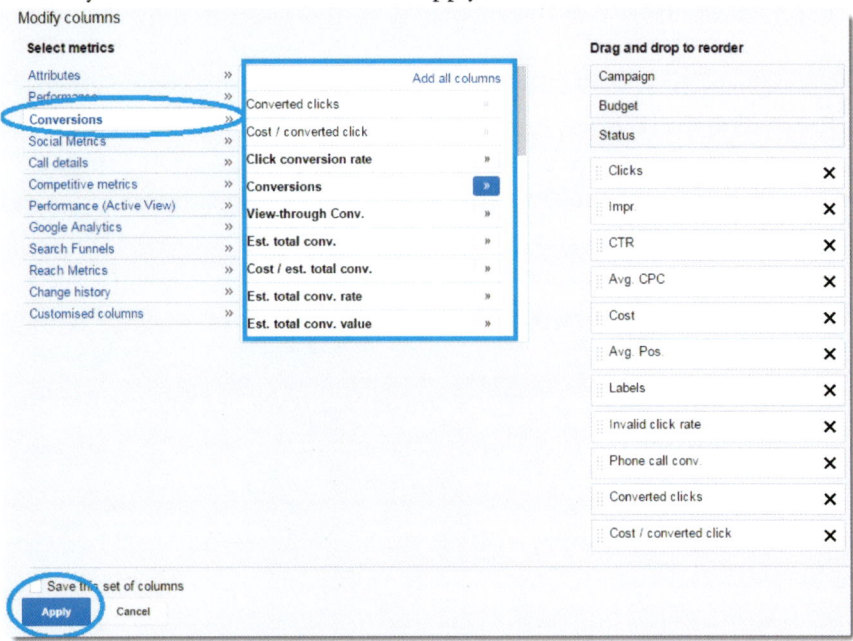

The new columns like these will appear to the right of your current columns.

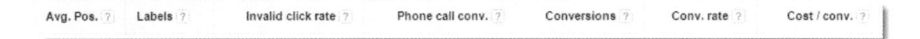

TIP: You'll need to do this, at all levels of your account, to see the details at each level.

Rapid Recap

- Conversion tracking is crucial – set it up before you send your AdWords campaign live so you can see what is happening and better optimise your campaigns over time!
- Conversion tracking is a great way to monitor your account and reveal which aspects are successful and which need more work. Follow the step by step method to install conversion tracking so you can see exactly where your money is going and what is making you money.
- Setting up 'Goals' in Google Analytics is also an option.
- Whichever option you use Google AdWords Conversion Tracking or Google Analytics Goals – implement tracking to make sure you can measure what is happening, that way you can take informed actions to improve your AdWords campaigns and landing pages.
- Don't forget to add the new reporting options via the Columns tab.

Chapter Checklist

- ✓ Go to the tools tab in AdWords and select 'Conversions' from the menu.
- ✓ Click on the button '+CONVERSION'.

New Conversion
- ✓ Select the source. If you're unsure go for 'Web page'.
- ✓ Name your conversion.

Settings
- ✓ Set your Conversion Value. To start select 'Each time it happens…' with the standard value of £1.
- ✓ Select 'All conversions' under the Count section.
- ✓ Set Conversion Window. The conversion windows vary from one industry to another, but if you're unsure go with '30 days'.
- ✓ For Conversion Category select 'Lead' or whatever is most appropriate for the action your website visitor has taken.

- ✓ Turn off the 'Optimisation' option.
- ✓ Review and decide whether you or someone else will add the code to your 'thank you' pages.
- ✓ Send the code to your Web Developer if necessary and ask them to place the code in the right place!

CHAPTER EIGHT
QUALITY SCORE

Quality Score is Google's way of rating your AdWords campaigns and landing pages. It determines how much you pay for clicks on your ads, as well as how high your adverts will appear on the Google search results page.

I've mentioned this briefly before but I cannot emphasise enough just how important your Quality Score is; a low quality score will cause your costs to rocket and your position on Google to plummet. But never fear, even if your Quality Score is bad to begin with there are ways of improving it dramatically!

Your Quality Score is calculated using a complicated algorithm created by Google to ensure that success on AdWords is achievable by all, not just those who can pay the most. This is where all that endless work you've done split testing, refining your campaign (if you've haven't, then shame on you) really comes into play. The better your campaign the better your Quality Score; the better your Quality Score the less you will pay.

How to Access Your Quality Score
To access your Quality Score, do the following:
1. Go to the 'Keyword' Tab.
2. Click 'Columns' > 'Customise Columns'.

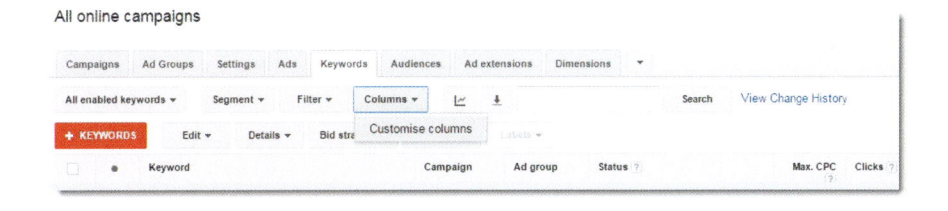

3. Attributes > Click Add next to 'Quality Score'.

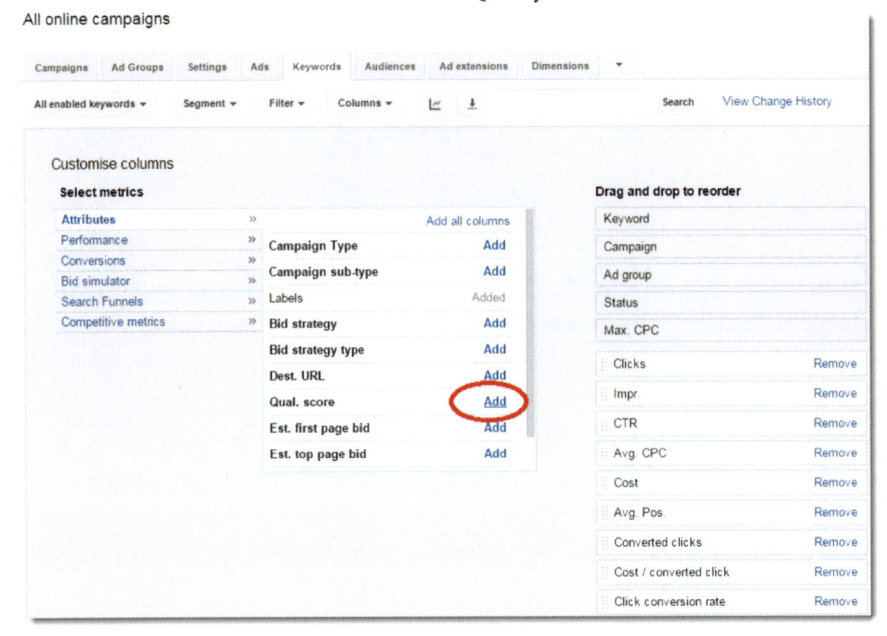

4. Click Apply.

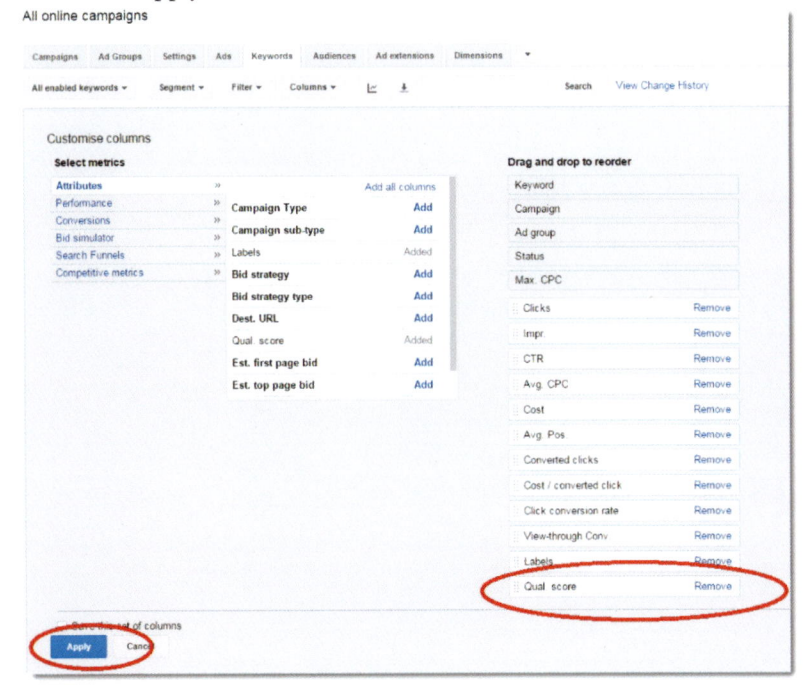

You should now be able to see your Quality Score in a column down the right hand side on your Keywords tab. The Quality Score is provided for every keyword in your campaign as shown below for my client, PWR Lettings.

Avg. Pos.	Converted clicks	Cost / converted click	Click conversion rate	View-through Conv.	Labels	Qual. score ↓
1.5	0	£0.00	0.00%	0		--
0.0	0	£0.00	0.00%	0	--	10/10
0.0	0	£0.00	0.00%	0	--	10/10
0.0	0	£0.00	0.00%	0	--	10/10
1.2	0	£0.00	0.00%	0	--	9/10
1.0	0	£0.00	0.00%	0	--	9/10
1.2	0	£0.00	0.00%	0	--	9/10

Understanding Your Quality Score

So you've been given a score out of 10, but what does that number actually mean?

Well, below are some guidelines as to what your score means and what you should do about it.

8-10 **Top marks!** Don't change a thing, your campaigns, keywords and ads are working perfectly and you are paying the least amount for them.

5-7 **Room for improvement**. You have the potential to make your campaigns even better, so go through it and try to spot any mistakes you've made along the way.

3-4 **Not so good.** Your campaign needs some serious TLC to get it working well for you. You're paying more than you should be for clicks. Look at your keywords to check their relevance to your Ad Groups and campaigns.

1-2 **Uh Oh**. Your ads are barely showing on Google; Google may not even show your adverts, and you're paying through the roof. Not good. You need to improve your campaigns and you need to do it now! We will explain what you can do in this chapter as well as chapter 9.

TIP: Google even gives you an idea of why your Quality Score is low. Hover over the speech bubble next to a keyword and you'll be given some advice from Google on what you need to work on to improve your score.

Here's an example of what you can expect when you hover over the speech bubble.

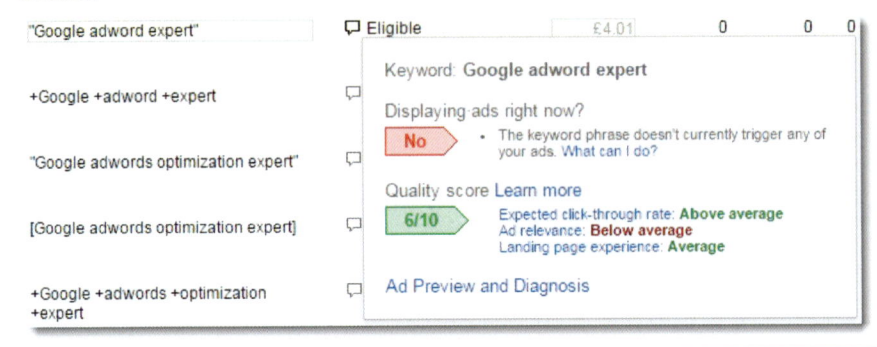

"Google adword expert"	Eligible	£4.01	0	0	0
+Google +adword +expert					
"Google adwords optimization expert"					
[Google adwords optimization expert]					
+Google +adwords +optimization +expert					

Keyword: Google adword expert
Displaying ads right now?
No — The keyword phrase doesn't currently trigger any of your ads. What can I do?
Quality score Learn more
6/10 — Expected click-through rate: **Above average**
Ad relevance: **Below average**
Landing page experience: **Average**
Ad Preview and Diagnosis

Needless to say, I got the issue sorted very quickly.

What Does Your Quality Score Assess?

Quality Score is based on several key aspects of your campaigns. These are:

- **CTR (Click Through Rate)**

As I said before, Google has kept the exact Quality Score equation under wraps, however we do know CTR is THE most important factor. Some people even speculate that it makes up for two-thirds of your Quality Score. Google wants to display ads that are relevant; if your ads are clicked on then they are considered relevant and will be shown. It is very hard to predict what a good CTR percentage is. Depending on your ad and its relevance, its position on Google and the level of the competition, you can achieve between 0.1% and 4.25%.[6] In fact I have clients like PWR Lettings who achieve click through rates as high as 26.24% so maybe 4.25% is a good initial objective.

TIP: Ads in the top 1% have a CTR six times higher than the average CTR for that product or service.[7]

- **Keywords**

Keywords form the basis of your campaigns and so it is crucial that they are not dumped into your campaigns without thought. Make sure you split your keywords into Ad Groups around themes – so all the phrases in an Ad Group are similar and relevant.

TIP: If necessary move keywords out of an Ad Group and set up a new Ad Group, as this is often the quickest way of improving your keywords' Quality Score. This technique is known as 'Peel and Stick'. I will be discussing this in the next chapter as it is such an important activity.

- **Landing Pages**

Google needs to see that your landing page is relevant to your keywords. Is it easy to navigate? Does it link well with your ad? Is it what someone clicking on your ad would expect? Look back to chapter 6 on landing pages and go through the advice I gave you to check you've ticked all the boxes.

- **Ad Text**

Again, this is a test of relevancy. Does your ad text match up to what the searcher wants and has keyed into Google? Can they see the keyword in the headline? Look back to the chapter on ad text, chapter 5, to see a breakdown of exactly what needs to be in your ad text.

- **AdWords Account Performance History**

You can't manually change this setting, but by ensuring your AdWords account is good from the start this shouldn't be too much of a problem.

Improving Your AdWords Campaigns to Improve Your Quality Score
- **Split Test to Improve Ads and Landing Pages**

You can test and improve almost every aspect of your campaigns by split testing your ads and landing pages to see which variations get more clicks and more conversion. You can never split test enough, especially when a key way of improving your Quality Score is to improve your CTR by reviewing your ads (and your message and offer). And don't forget conversion rates too.

- **Improve Your Individual Keyword Quality Score**

Quality Score measures the success of each and every keyword in your campaign. With this in mind, make sure you give equal attention to the keywords in every Ad Group. If you have one Ad Group with well researched and relevant keywords, that's great but if the rest or even just one of your Ad Groups has inadequate, poorly thought out keywords, your Quality Score overall will be affected. Ensure this doesn't happen by grouping your keywords in themes - roughly 5-10 in each Ad Group and only use keywords which are entirely relevant to your ads and what you're selling. If you have keywords with low Quality Scores consider taking them out of the Ad Group and setting up a new Ad Group specifically for those phrases. This is 'Peel and Stick'.

- **Landing Pages**

As I made clear in the last chapter, landing pages are extremely important when it comes to securing your customer. If you're suffering with a Quality Score below four, it may be due to your landing page, so go back over the checklist I gave you in chapter 6 and be sure that everything is in order. Make sure your landing page reflects your keywords and what's in your ads.

So there you have it; you can now see your Quality Scores and I've shown you what to look for to help improve them. It's now essential that you to go through your campaigns and Ad Groups and make the necessary alterations to increase your Quality Scores.

Why Quality Score is Crucial!

I've already stated that a low Quality Score will increase costs, but just to make sure you've got the message, take a look at this great infographic from our friends at WordStream.

Quality Score affects your CPC

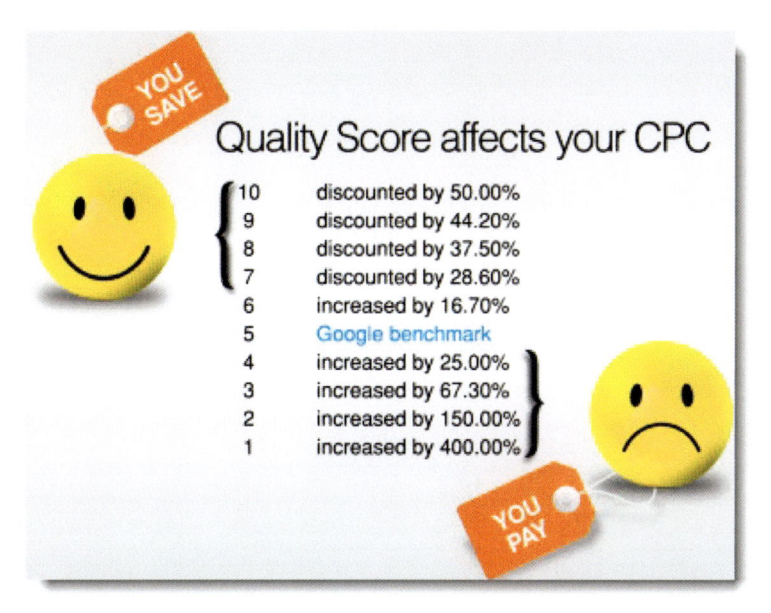

10	discounted by 50.00%
9	discounted by 44.20%
8	discounted by 37.50%
7	discounted by 28.60%
6	increased by 16.70%
5	Google benchmark
4	increased by 25.00%
3	increased by 67.30%
2	increased by 150.00%
1	increased by 400.00%

As you can see unless your Quality Scores are high, you'll be paying more than you need to, that's why it is so important. If you don't want to pay over the odds, take note of your Quality Scores and improve them!

Rapid Recap

- Quality Score is the score out of ten which determines your ads ranking and your cost per click.
- Your Quality Score assesses five key aspects of your campaign: CTR, Keywords, Landing Page, Ad Text and Performance History, so make sure each part of your campaign is just as good as the next – it only takes one aspect to bring your Quality Score down.
- If your Quality Score is initially abysmal, you should take action immediately. There are three ports of call which you need to visit immediately to boost your score; check each keyword and find out why it has a low score (hover over the speech bubble next to the keyword). You may need to move the keyword/s to a new Ad Group with an ad written specifically for it, check your adverts and your landing page.
- Despite the risk of me sounding like a broken record, keep split testing adverts and landing pages.

CHAPTER NINE
CAMPAIGN OPTIMISATION

Why Campaign Optimisation?
There are many mistakes Google AdWords newbies, inexperienced users or people without the proper training make with their AdWords account, but one of the things I see time and time again when I get asked to help with an AdWords campaign is that the company has set a campaign up and just let it run. No thought to improving it, optimising it, learning from the data or tweaking anything.

To get the best out of Google AdWords, it is vital to understand that it is a work in progress. You don't just set it up in a day and leave it to work its magic – you need to be constantly checking and refining your campaigns. Google is good for a lot of things but it certainly won't do this for you.

Now don't be dis-heartened by this – over time you will be able to spend less and less time on the activities I'm going to outline, but initially you should expect to spend at least a few hours a week tweaking and making various improvements. Once you feel your campaigns have been optimised to their maximum potential you can sit back and relax a bit more, perhaps only checking your account for 2-3 hours per month to ensure everything is on track.

Throughout your time using AdWords, you always need to check three key things; that you are not wasting any money, that you are improving click through rates and that you are improving conversion rates - ultimately reducing your cost per conversion. Below are six key optimising activities that you should be performing on a regular basis.

1.   Search Terms All Report and Its Use
This is a crucial activity that should be performed on a daily, weekly or monthly basis depending on your spend/the number of clicks you have in a given month; the more clicks the more regularly you should look at and

perform actions based on this report. I certainly recommend doing it weekly initially, or even daily if you have the time and are generating plenty of clicks each day. Effectively the more often you do this, the less money you will waste on unwanted clicks.

To find the Search Terms All Report, you have to go to the Keyword tab – either at campaign level or Ad Group level. I'd suggest you start by looking at each Ad Group individually, but as time goes by campaign level will be fine.

To start, go to the first campaign and first Ad Group, go to the Keywords tab and Click 'Details', SEARCH TERMS, 'All' as shown below:

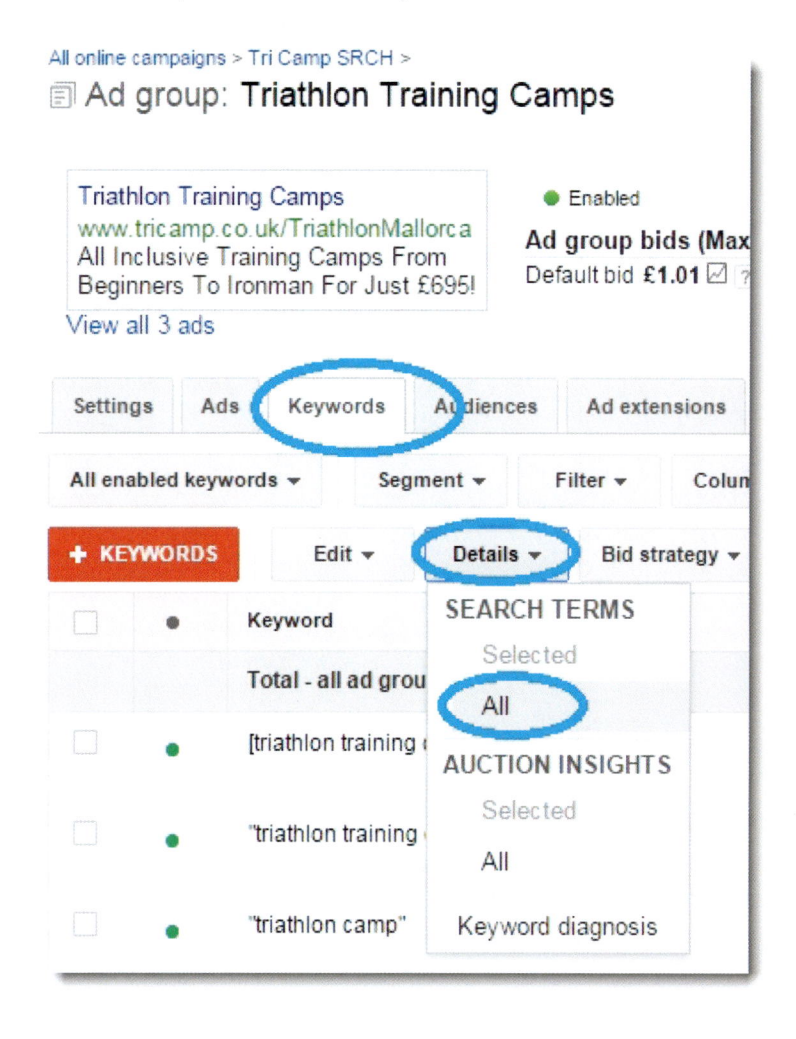

When you click on 'All', you'll be presented with a screen like this:

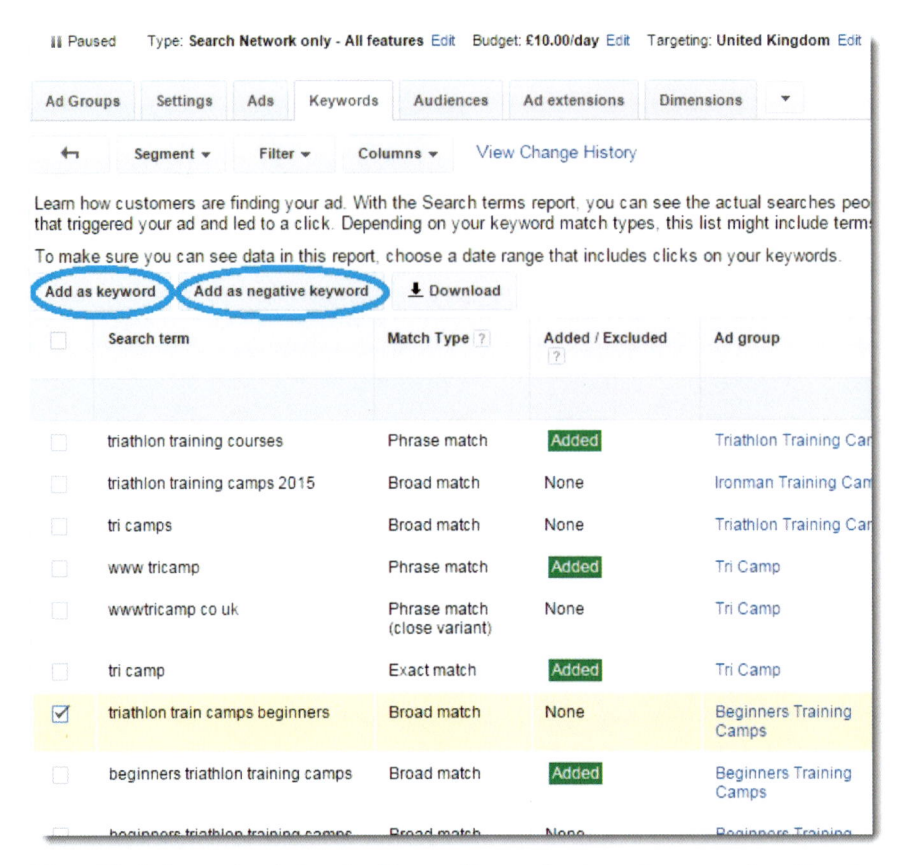

[Screenshot of Google AdWords Keywords tab showing search terms report with 'Add as keyword' and 'Add as negative keyword' buttons circled. The table shows search terms including: triathlon training courses (Phrase match, Added, Triathlon Training Cam), triathlon training camps 2015 (Broad match, None, Ironman Training Cam), tri camps (Broad match, None, Triathlon Training Cam), www tricamp (Phrase match, Added, Tri Camp), wwwtricamp co uk (Phrase match close variant, None, Tri Camp), tri camp (Exact match, Added, Tri Camp), triathlon train camps beginners (Broad match, None, Beginners Training Camps), beginners triathlon training camps (Broad match, Added, Beginners Training Camps).]

Now this information is invaluable to all organisations that are using Google AdWords. It tells you exactly what you have been found for and as such it gives you the opportunity to review each Search Term to decide whether you would want to be found for that phrase again. You can either 'Add as keyword' or 'Add as negative keyword'.

There may be some really obvious ones to add as negatives and some that are just what you want and very relevant. As you can see from the image above, I've added phrases already as shown by the green 'Added' symbol. NOTE: When adding keywords, don't add them as Broad; change them to Broad Match Modified or Exact where appropriate.

Probably most importantly this report is vital for building your negative keyword list. This process effectively keeps your costs down and improves your cost per conversion as it helps you to identify those words that you don't want to be found for. As an example you might want to be found for 'drum lessons Nottingham' but not 'cheap drum lessons Nottingham' so cheap is added as a negative.

TIP: To prioritise your work, sort the Campaigns by Clicks and the Ad Groups by Clicks and you'll be able to start with the Ad Groups that have the most data and work down the list.

TIP: The Search Terms All Report is also great for finding new keywords that convert as you can also see which keywords led to conversions if you have conversion tracking sorted.

2. <u>The Peel and Stick Process</u>
So what is Peel and Stick?

When reviewing your keywords within an Ad Group, if there is one particular keyword with a low Quality Score, you should remove it from the Ad Group it's in and create a new Ad Group with an ad that is more relevant to that keyword. You will instantly see an improvement in its Quality Score; this is the Peel and Stick method.

How to do this;
    i)   Well for starters, find that keyword which isn't performing so well and needs its own Ad Group. In the below example you can see me performing this process with one of my clients, Funkyfones.

Avg. Pos. [?]	Converted clicks [?]	Cost / converted click [?]	Click conversion rate [?]	View-through Conv. [?]	Labels [?]	Qual. ↑ score [?]
1.5	27	£134.89	0.57%	0	--	--
1.8	0	£0.00	0.00%	0	--	3/10

You can see here the Quality Score for this particular phrase is too low.

ii) You need to set up the new Ad Group for the keyword with the low quality score.

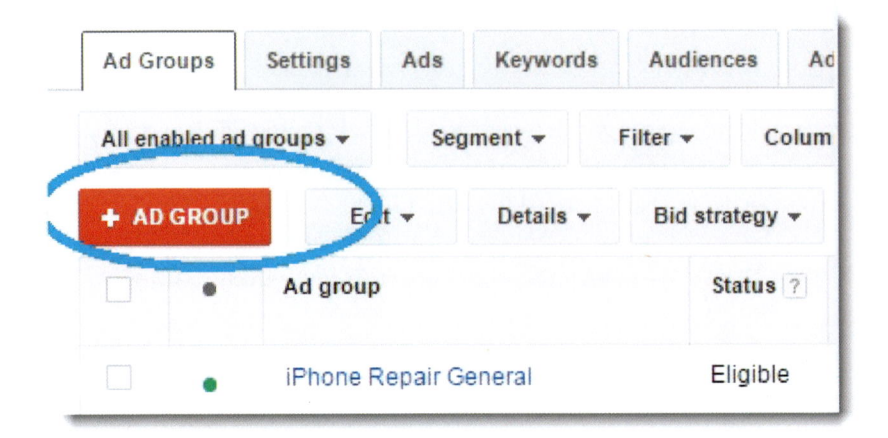

iii) Create your ad similarly to how you have done previously. Make sure that the ad text and headline match well to the keyword and that the keyword is entered into the keywords box as an exact match (using square brackets). I've chosen Exact because the keyword I'm moving over is Broad Match Modified (with the + before each word). See illustration over the page.

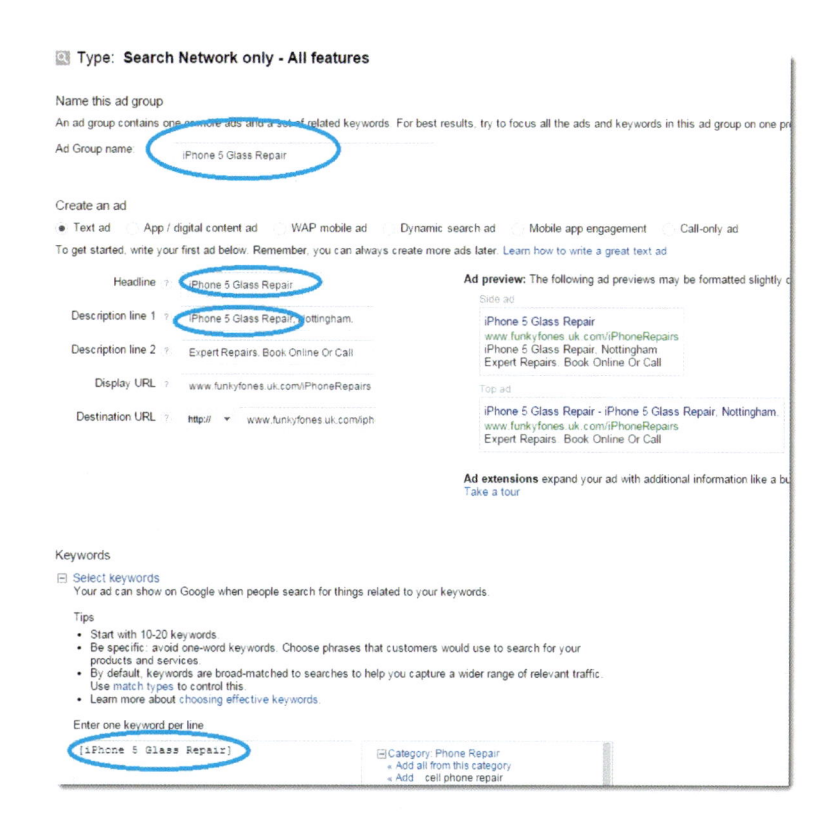

iv) Now go back to your original phrase and select 'Edit' then 'copy'.

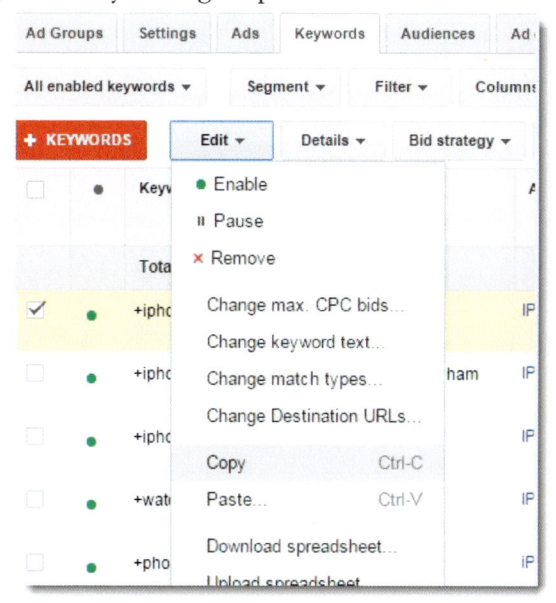

Then go to your new Ad Group, select 'Edit' and then 'Paste'.

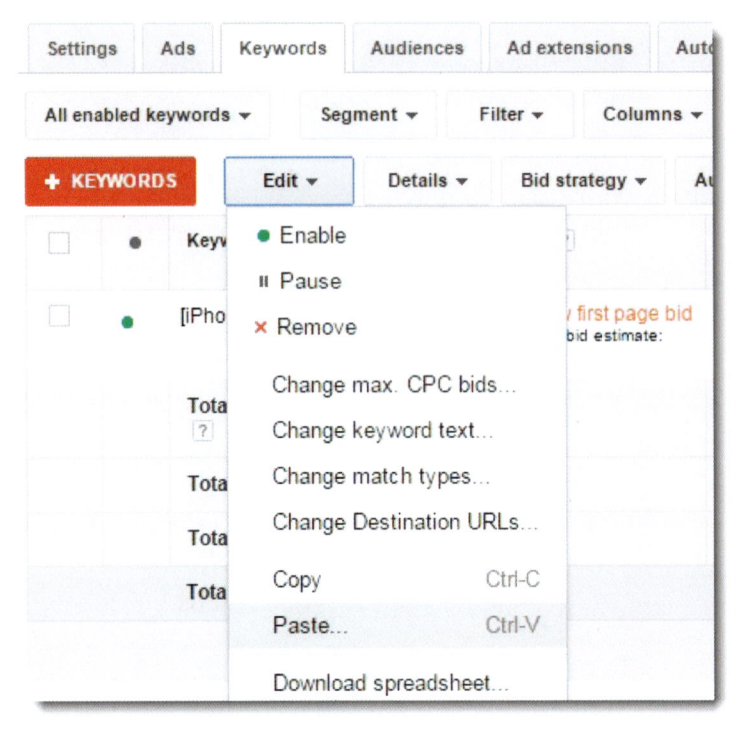

v) Before you can paste, Google gives you three tick boxes which you must look at before you paste. I recommend ticking 'Include bids' but NOT ticking the other two; 'Include destination URL's' and 'Pause new keywords after pasting'.

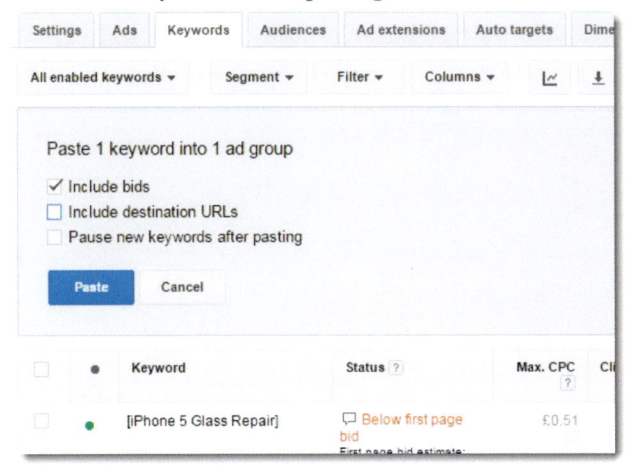

vi) This next step is absolutely crucial. You must now go back and pause the keyword you have moved/copied, otherwise you are essentially competing against yourself which obviously, is rather pointless and a waste of money!

vii) Once you've done this go to your new Ad Group and create more ads.

Avg. Pos.	Converted clicks	Cost / converted click	Click conversion rate	View-through Conv.	Labels	Qual. score ↑
0	0	£0.00	0.00%	0	--	5/10
0.0	0	£0.00	0.00%	0	--	6/10
0.0	0	£0.00	0.00%	0		--

You can see here how simple Peel and Stick is and also how much it can improve your Quality Score. In this case, we improved it from a 3 to a 5 simply by moving it into an Ad Group of its own.

It might be easier to see this process in video form, so there will be a video on the Peel and Stick process in the Google AdWords Academy Course at www.jackie-key.com.

3. Removing Zero Impression Keywords

After a period of around two to three months, it is worth removing keywords that have had no impressions – in other words, no one is searching for that phrase. If they aren't searching for it, it is best to pause or even delete it. By doing this you will improve the click through rates of your campaigns and Ad Groups. And as a good click through rate is something Google likes and forms part of your overall Quality Score, it is certainly worth doing.

Simply sort your keywords by impressions and pause the ones with zero impressions – unless you've recently added them or moved them using the Peel and Stick method described previously.

4. Optimising Bids

It is possible to look at your bids and adjust them at both Ad Group level and keyword level. Initially you might want to look to increase the bids on all the keywords in an Ad Group, perhaps when all keywords are in a low position, so you should adjust the bid at the Ad Group level in this situation.

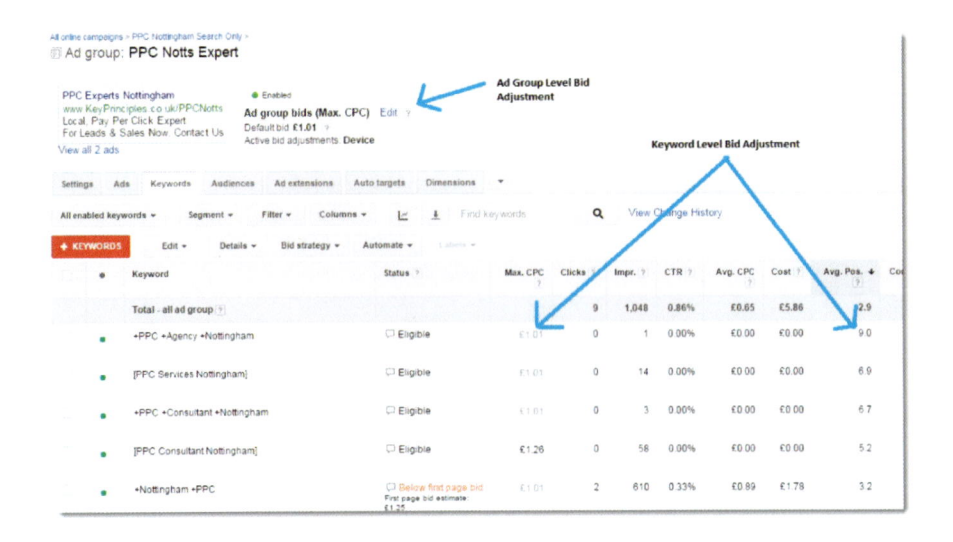

However as you start to see what is working and what isn't you can start to adjust bids at the keyword level. If budgets are tight I'd suggest you look at bid adjustment at keyword level sooner rather than later.

Also, before you even think about increasing bids, take a look at your Quality Scores and see if they need improving. If you're happy with it, check the position your keyword is achieving over all time, but also after your most recent review of bids. You don't want to increase bids too quickly or by too much. Ideally you would want to aim between 2 and 3 for an average position (assuming your budget makes this possible).

TIP: Google sometimes includes 'Below first page bid' in orange and suggests a first page bid estimate. Be careful as sometimes this can be misleading. Sometimes the average position can be much better, even 2 or 3. So don't automatically increase your bid prices when you see the 'Below first page' alert – check what your average position is first! Below is an example of this for PWR Lettings where Google is suggesting I increase the bid prices even though the average positions are 1.0 and 2.4 respectively.

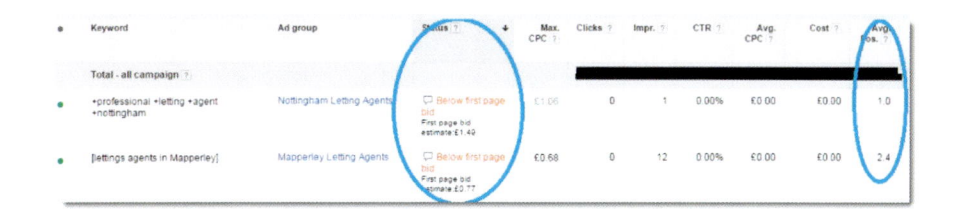

Keyword	Ad group	Status	Max. CPC	Clicks	Impr.	CTR	Avg. CPC	Cost	Avg. Pos.
Total - all campaign									
+professional +letting +agent +nottingham	Nottingham Letting Agents	Below first page bid First page bid estimate £1.49	£1.06	0	1	0.00%	£0.00	£0.00	1.0
[lettings agents in Mapperley]	Mapperley Letting Agents	Below first page bid First page bid estimate £0.77	£0.68	0	12	0.00%	£0.00	£0.00	2.4

You also need to think about the maximum bid price you are prepared to pay. You need to be aiming for a return on investment. Think about the lifetime value of the customer (as discussed in Chapter 2), your cost per click and the conversion rates that you are starting to achieve. Can you afford to increase your bids or do you need to look at improving Quality Scores and conversion rates first?

Bid optimisation is an important activity. You may want to increase your bid price for keywords that are performing well to achieve a better position and perhaps even reduce bids for lower performing keywords. You could even 'pause' those underperforming keywords to concentrate on the ones that are providing the best return.

As you start to see the data come through, you'll be able to make informed decisions on what is required - as long as you have your conversion tracking set up.

TIP: If you get more calls once you start your AdWords campaign, it is a good idea to also set up a tracking number for your AdWords campaigns so you can see exactly what is being generated from this marketing channel. In fact, it is best to have individual call tracking numbers for each marketing channel, so that you can truly measure where your leads and ultimately sales are coming from and then adjust your spend in those channels accordingly, based on hard facts rather than a gut feeling.

5. <u>Advert Improvements</u>

If you have the adverts running on a 'Rotate Indefinitely' or for '90 days' as outlined in Chapter 4, you'll be able to clearly identify the winners and losers in your split testing battle. Put simply, pause the advert/s with the lower click through rate and set up new adverts to see if you can beat the best performing advert. You want to improve your click through rate as time goes on, but also make sure you look at conversion rates too – you don't want to pause an advert that is providing high conversion rates. There may be situations where it is tricky to know which to turn off, but it should be based on your overall campaign objectives.

TIP: Make sure you have a reasonable number of impressions before deciding one advert is much better than another. Don't be too hasty dropping an advert. Give them at least 200 impressions worth of time; give them a chance to show what they can do.

6. Landing Pages

We've had a whole chapter on landing pages so I won't say much more here – other than split test landing pages. This is where you can make the greatest impact on conversion rates (other than reviewing your offer completely – which may be required if your conversion rates are too low).

Tweaks to landing pages can certainly help with conversion rates and also help improve Quality Scores. It may even be appropriate to set up new landing pages for specific Ad Groups that are performing particularly well to improve Quality Scores and conversion rates further.

You can always be making improvements to your AdWords campaigns with the aim of reducing costs and improving cost per conversion. There's a lot more on this in my online course when you are ready to go for further optimisation techniques.

Rapid Recap

- Just because you have finished the set up stage of your campaign and Ad Groups does not mean your work is done. Think of your AdWords account as your baby; you can't just create it and then shove it out into the world; it needs plenty of tender love and care if it is to succeed!
- Using Search Terms All Report you find out what you've been found for. It is a crucial part of regular optimisation. In particular, use the results to add to your list of negatives.

- The Peel and Stick Process helps you to increase the Quality Score of your keywords by placing them in new Ad Groups.
- Always make sure you keep an eye on the statistics of your keywords and remove those which have had zero impressions after 60 or 90 days.
- Bid optimisation is crucial if your account is to take off. You can monitor your bids at the Ad Group level and alter them as a group, or individually at keyword level, depending on their success. Always keep in mind the value of your potential customer when deciding your bids; it's better to pay a little more than you want to get the customer than not get the customer at all.
- Landing pages are a key part of your campaign. They need to be relevant to your keywords so they affect your Quality Scores in a positive way as well as provide conversions, leads and sales. Always split test and even create new landing pages for campaigns and Ad Groups that are performing particularly well and especially if they have high search volumes, a high number of clicks but low conversion rates.

Chapter Checklist
Campaign Optimisation
1. **Search Terms All Report**
    - Go to your first Ad Group within your first campaign, click on the keywords tab, click 'Details, SEARCH TERMS, 'All'.
    - Go through the list that appears, and 'Add as Keyword' or 'Add as Negative keyword' as appropriate.
2. **Peel and Stick**
    - Find an underperforming keyword which differs from the rest in the Ad Group.
    - Set up a new Ad Group.
    - Create a new ad (making sure the ad text and headline relate closely to the keyword).
    - Go back to the original keyword, select 'Edit', 'Copy', then return to the new group and select 'Edit', 'Paste'.
    - A box will appear before you can paste. Click the first option 'Include bids' but leave the next two options unticked.

- ✓ Now go back and PAUSE THE ORIGINAL KEYWORD.
- ✓ Go to your new Ad Group and create more ads.
- ✓ Do this over and over to improve your Quality Scores especially for phrases that have high search volumes.

3. **Zero Impressions**
   - ✓ Remove, either delete or pause, keywords that have zero impressions after 60 or 90 days.

4. **Bid Optimisation**
   - ✓ For high performing keywords, consider increasing your maximum cost per click if you need to improve your average position.
   - ✓ For low performing keywords, consider improving their position if needed or alternatively reduce bids or pause them completely.

5. **Advert Improvements**
   - ✓ Keep split testing your adverts with the aim of improving click through rates and conversion rates.

6. **Landing Pages**
   - ✓ Split test landing pages with the aim of improving conversion rates.
   - ✓ Consider new landing pages for keywords that have large volumes of searches and clicks so you can improve conversion rates.
   - ✓ Low conversions rates? Consider what you are offering and whether you need to change the offer in some way, whether it is the message, the price or some other factor.

Chapter Ten
Other Google Networks

The power of using other networks to host your ad is a potentially huge asset which can gain you valuable leads and sales. However if not managed correctly using the other networks can be equivalent of throwing money down the drain. This chapter will introduce you to using Google's Display Network (GDN) and show you how to maximise your chances of coming out on top.

What is the Google Display Network?

We first came across the option to use GDN at the very beginning of your AdWords journey. At the time, I told you to stick to Google's Search Network only as it means we have much more control.

However, you can set up separate campaigns within your Google AdWords account that focus on the GDN only. By doing this, you can place an ad on websites totally separate from Google, that have agreed to allow Google's advertisers to place adverts on their site. By doing this you'll instantly see an increase in traffic and potentially more conversions as Google's Display Network includes over two million websites.

How Does It Work?

Previously advertising on a multitude of difference sites would have been more effort than it was worth. Now Google has made this option far more accessible to the small business owner by essentially doing all the legwork for you. You don't have to find the right sites yourself, you don't have to consult the owner of the site and negotiate prices, instead you just use the GDN and Google will act as the middle man between you 'the advertiser' and the website owner 'the producer'.

The process begins with the producer wanting to make some money out of their website. They place a code on their website, which allows Google a space to place advertisements. Google places your ad on the site. You, the advertiser, pays Google if a visitor to the website with your advert on it, clicks on your advert and goes to your website. The amount you pay Google is then split between Google and the producer.

As ever whilst Google is acting as the middle man, it retains most of the power in the relationship, as the producer has very little control over the ads which will appear on their site. However as I will go on to explain, you have to decide just how much control you want to hand over to Google.

Search VS Display - Which Does What?

SEARCH NETWORK	DISPLAY NETWORK
• Search Network only shows your ads on the Google search results page (and partners if you left that ticked).	• Your ad will appear on all sorts of sites, over two million sites in fact, so the list is endless.
• Limits audience to only those who use Google's search engine.	• Your reach is far broader, at a whopping 93% of the internet.
• Very controlled template for your advert – limited number of words (and image if you use Google Shopping).	• You can build creative adverts, using colours, images and even movement.
• When your ad appears on the Google search results page, it is directly linked to what the searcher entered into Google. They are in searching mode and so your ad will be welcome.	• Your ads will appear when people aren't searching so they may be seen as an annoyance rather than helpful.
	• You can target an audience based on its interest as shown by their Google history.
	• You are able to take advantage of free apps for mobiles and tablets.

How to Choose Who to Target

Should you opt to take advantage of the GDN, Google offers you varying levels of control over who you are targeting with your ad. I find it helpful to think of these levels as different stages of a funnel; the beginning being the narrowest part allowing through only a limited amount, progressing to the largest part allowing in the most.

Whichever approach you choose for your GDN campaign, Google will allow your ad to be available to a different amount of sites. The narrower you choose your funnel to be the fewer sites will display your ads.

At the larger end of the funnel is **Topic Targeting**. This option allows Google to become more involved. Google will give you the option of selecting a topic for which you want your ad to appear.

The range of topics is extensive so there's no way your product or service won't fit in somewhere.

- ✓ With this option you can target people who are on sites related to your ad.
- ✗ You will not be targeting the people of that given industry just the ones who happen to be looking at it. This method is still quite broad.

Next is **Keyword Targeting.** Similar to Topic Targeting but more specific as it focuses on a keyword or keywords which you provide Google and from which Google decides on sites appropriate for your adverts.

Narrower still is **Behavioural Targeting**. This is where Google actually get a little bit scary. By monitoring each of its users Google has built up millions of individual profiles which it can match to your ad by seeing whether they've searched for similar things in the past.

- ✓ You're still letting Google deploy your ad to maximum potential, but it's so specific, only showing your ads to the people who will appreciate them the most.
- ✗ It is slightly creepy…

Finally at the most controlled level, you have **Managed Placement Targeting.** Here, you hold all the cards. You, and only you, pick out the websites which you want to appear on giving Google very little say in the matter.

- ✓ This is great because there is no chance you'll be leaking money without realising.
- ✗ But it massively limits your potential reach as no matter how long you spend enabling your ad to be shown on different sites, you'll never cover the amount which Google could in a second.

So there are your four options, now which one to go for..?

For a small business owner I'd recommend going for one of the middle options. It's best not to be too restrained when using GDN or else it sort of defeats the point of using it. But at the same time, you can't afford the expense of making a mistake on GDN as larger companies can, so don't be too haphazard with your settings.

Setting Your Bidding Options

1) **CPC – Cost per click.** You've heard of this before as this is the setting you use on the AdWords Search campaigns. You only pay when people click on your advert.
2) **CPM – Cost per impressions.** With this method you pay for Google to show your ad 1000 times regardless of whether it is clicked on or not.
3) **CPA – Cost per action.** This option is only available if you have been using GDN for while already - you need at least 15 conversions per day within 30 days. Google measures how much you pay on how good a match your ad is to what the searcher wants. Google will charge more if you're likely to convert, less if you're not or perhaps even hide the ad altogether.

For most small businesses, I would recommend CPC bidding and of course you can set a daily budget for this campaign in your AdWords account, just like you can do with your AdWords Search campaign.

How to Succeed at Interruption Marketing

When you're advertising on GDN you are essentially an unwanted interruption. In today's world we are bombarded with adverts; on TV, the internet, radio and so it's something we learn to live with and tune out if we can.

Occasionally however there are exceptions, ads that stand out and become hits, circling the internet via social media. Now I'm not saying that you will be able to create such a phenomenon, but the key thing to note here is that the ads which succeed are the ads which have the ability to hook the viewer in. You need something to grab the attention of your potential customer, not just an interesting feature, but a juicy offer that they'll really want to get their teeth into.

So what to offer..?

Of course it does depend on your business, but no matter what you are trying to sell you can always apply one of the universally acknowledged facts of life; nothing looks, tastes or feels better than when it's free. So give them a freebie, be it a PDF download, a taster of your product, or a coupon. If you supply this freebie with no strings attached, other than a data capture form, then if you're targeting the right audience you're sure to get clicks.

Remarketing on GDN

Remarketing is yet another way to use GDN to your advantage. Remarketing allows you to target customers who once showed interest in your company by visiting your website, but failed to follow through, i.e. they didn't buy your product or service or leave any contact details.

Remarketing gives you the ability to follow that customer round the internet placing your advert on the pages they visit in order to prompt them to return to your website and take an action. Yes, I know what you're thinking... essentially you are stalking your potential customer, but don't worry, it's definitely legal!

Remarketing is especially great for those of you whose product is expensive or is something that your customer is likely to want to put off, like writing a will for example. Using this method of marketing means, in some industries, you're 70% more likely to gain a lead or sale than you would without it. Other benefits include increasing brand awareness, making you look bigger than you are and you can even encourage those who have already made a purchase to make a further purchase by advertising other products or services.

I use it for Key Principles and here is an example of Remarketing in action.

Many of my clients use Google Remarketing to encourage return visits including PWR Lettings. Below is a perfectly placed text version of their Remarketing advert on the UK Letting Agents Directory – great placement as they are a letting agent!

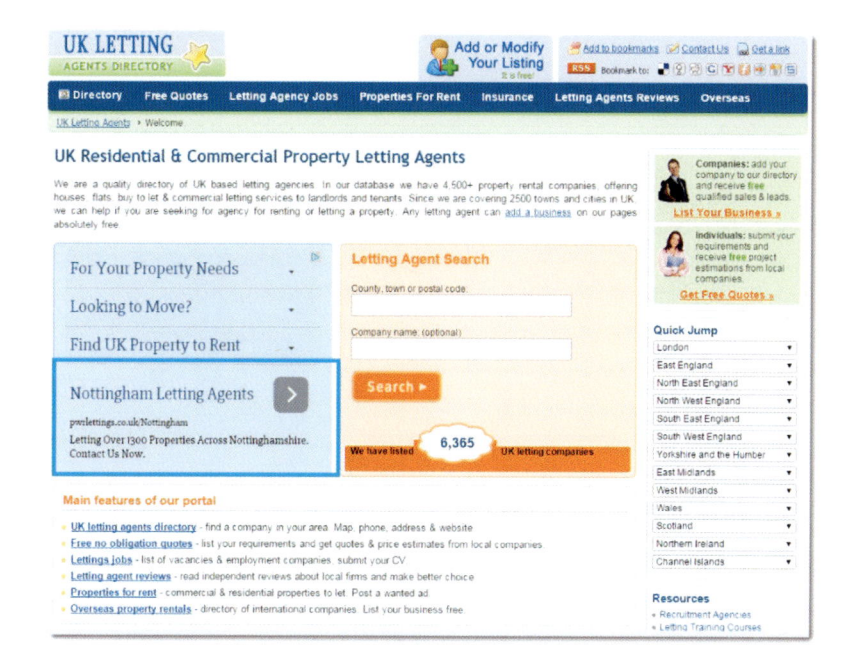

Rapid Recap

➢ Google's Display Network allows you to place your ads on websites other than Google. This massively increases your base for attracting potential customers and increases brand awareness.

➢ Whilst this sounds particularly daunting you can control where your ads appear using several settings; Topic, Keyword, Behavioural and Management Placement Targeting.

➢ Just like Google search campaigns, you can set a daily budget with Google for GDN campaigns too.

➢ When using GDN you are using a particular type of marketing – Interruption Marketing. The internet browser is not actually looking for your product or service. You have to make your ad extra enticing in order to get them to click on your advert and visit your website.

➢ Remarketing is a way of getting back visitors to your website who showed an interest in your company by visiting, but didn't convert to customers. This form of advertising can be very effective at increasing conversion rates.

HERE'S TO YOUR SUCCESS WITH GOOGLE ADWORDS!

The task of providing a conclusion on how to use Google AdWords is virtually impossible, with AdWords being such a multifaceted tool, it's hard to summarise it in only a few paragraphs. So instead of attempting to do that, I've drawn out 10 key points from my 10 chapters in order to provide an, albeit basic, but fairly complete picture of how a small business owner can successfully use Google AdWords.

1. For the small business owner AdWords is a both a strategic and tactical game; each action needs to be well researched and thought out. If you are to succeed you need to remember three key things; find a niche, specify a location and be relevant!

2. The work you do before you begin with AdWords is equally as important as the work you do when actually setting it up. AdWords requires you and your company to be at the top of your game so when potential customers do start to notice you, you are ready to receive them. You need to do your research, have a domain, website and shopping cart before you're ready to go, as well as most importantly know why someone would come to you over your competition.

3. Thorough keyword research is crucial to a successful campaign. Before you even begin to think about setting up your Ad Groups and adverts, you need to have a clear idea of what your keywords are going to be and how you are going to group them. Don't forget your Negative keywords – these are crucial in that they actually save you money.

4. When setting up your account, just follow the steps at a steady pace and be meticulous when it comes to Google's pre-selected settings – they are often not the best options. And don't worry too much, these settings can be altered and you can even pause your first campaign if you're worried it's not right for you.

5. Your adverts may make up only a small part of your account but your advert is essentially your front man; bringing in your potential customers and therefore all your leads and sales you make using AdWords, so make it good. Each line has a different purpose and you need to ensure that it fulfils it.

6. Landing pages are the next step in drawing in your customer so make them relevant, easy to navigate and not too pushy!

7. It is so important to track your progress when using AdWords, be it using Google AdWords Conversion Tracking or Google Analytics Goals. You need to know what's working and what's not so that you can work on making your campaign the best it can be, thus reducing your costs and improving your cost per conversion.

8. Your Quality Score assesses five key aspects of your campaign: CTR, Keywords, Landing Page, Ad Text and Performance History, so make sure each part of your campaign is just as good as the next – it only takes one aspect to bring your Quality Score down.

9. Always be refining your campaign. The longer your account has been live the less you need to check up on it, but that doesn't mean desert it all together. At least once a month you should look at Search Terms All Report (and more often if you're spending a large sum of money with Google), 'Peel and Stick' to improve the Quality Score of your keywords, whilst also look at bid optimisation and your landing page too. And of course there's the all-important split testing.

10. Google's Display Network is a great way of expanding your potential for bringing in new customers and getting back those prospects that showed interest, but didn't convert to customers. By targeting pages, other than Google Search, you'll have to employ a different type of marketing known as interruption marketing, but once you've mastered this and the knack of Remarketing you'll see the benefits roll in.

So there you have it. I hope I've made it clear throughout the course of this book how invaluable AdWords is as a tool for cracking open the goldmine that is the advertising potential of Google and the internet. You now have a fully-fledged AdWords account which should already be beginning to bring in extra profit, and from here it's onwards and upwards as your account continues to take off.

But, if you only take one thing from reading this book, let it be this; no matter what your product, income or goal, there is room for pretty much everyone on Google AdWords, and it would be simply illogical not to become a player in the game where everyone can be a winner.

If you're hungry for more information and want to continue to improve your AdWords campaigns, expand on your current success and develop your AdWords skills further, check out my course, the Google AdWords Academy at www.jackie-key.com. Remember as a valued reader of this book, you can secure a 25% discount at the checkout by including MANUAL when prompted for the promotional code. Please do not hesitate to contact me via my website www.jackie-key.com. I'd love to hear from you.

THE BIG LESSON

TRY IT

START SMALL

TEST, TEST, TEST

THE BOTTOM LINE

People are online, in your area, looking for what you have to offer, so it makes sense that you should be there when they are looking!

(If you aren't there, your competitors will be and they'll be getting the lion's share of the new business.)

Appendix

Power Words

Here are some words that can help your advert stand out from the crowd. Use them and see how your click through rates improve over time.

Advanced	Learn
Boost	New
Claim	Now
Create	Opportunity
Crucial	Painless
Dare	Proven
Demand	Reduce
Desire	Reveal
Discover	Save
Dreams	Secret
Eliminate	Start
Enable	Tactics
Exclusive	Targets
Free	Trust
Gain	Truth
Great	Try
Guarantee	Ultimate
Increase	Unique
Insist	Win
Invest	You

NEGATIVE WORDS TO CONSIDER

Below is a list of words which quite often fall into the category of negative keywords. BUT, you should not just take a selection of these and shove them into an Ad Group. Your negative keywords will be unique to your campaign, so whilst you can use these you need to sanity check them as well as come up with your own for your particular product or service.

About	Imported
Bargain	Job
Budget	Jobs
Career	Journal
Cheap	Picture
Classes	Photo
Course	Regulations
CV	Retail
Discount	Rules
Employer	Salary
Employment	Sale
Examples	Scheme
Explain	Template
File	Training
Forum	Tutorial
Free	Used
Guide	Vacancies
Handmade	Vacancy
Hiring	Vintage
Homemade	Wage
"How to"	"What is"
Image	"Where is"

GLOSSARY

Ad Extension - This is a feature which you can use to increase the size of your advert. Extra information about your business is displayed below your main advert on the search results page. There are several different types; Call Extensions, Location Extensions, Sitelink Extensions, etc.

Ad Group - These are created within your campaigns. You may have several individual ads in each Ad Group which target a similar set of keywords.

App Extension - An extension used when advertising on mobile or tablet. This extension allows you to link to the App store.

Ad Rank - This is a value used to position your ad on the Google search results page. The Ad Rank is measured by your CPC and Quality Score.

Broad Match - When you set a keyword as broad this means if any word in your targeted phrase is related to a search being made, your ad will appear. (Broad match is generally not recommended.)

Broad Match Modified - You set this up so that at least one word or even each word in your phrase has a + sign before it. With Broad Match Modified, you have more control than with Broad Match. You are specifying that you advert will trigger only when the searcher includes the keyword terms or their close variants. Close variants include misspellings, singular/plural forms, abbreviations and acronyms, and stemmings such as "fish" and "fishing".

Call Extensions - An extension of your ad that allows your searchers to call you directly from the ad. This costs the same as a click on your ad when someone calls.

Campaign - The level below account level is the campaign level. You can run several campaigns at the same time, each advertising their own product or service. Within a campaign there are Ad Groups.

Click Through Rate (CTR) - This is how many people clicked your ad when it appeared on their Google search results page compared to how many people have seen it. It's shown as a percentage - you should aim for a CTR of 5.0% or higher.

Clicks - This is the number of people that have clicked on your Google AdWords ad.

Conversions - This is the amount of times your goal has been completed after someone has clicked on your ad. For example asked for a quote, downloaded a white paper, got in contact or purchased from you.

Conversion Tracking - This is a tool available in AdWords which allows you to track your progress e.g. number of conversions. To activate Conversion Tracking you must insert code, which is added to the page which is shown after a conversion has been made. For example a thank you page after a purchase. (You can also set up goals in Google Analytics.)

Cost - This is how much you have spent with Google during a set period.

Cost Per Action/Acquisition (CPA) - This is how much you are willing to pay per conversion.

Cost Per Click (CPC) - You pay per click on your advert and you decide how much you are prepared to pay per click by setting a maximum cost per click.

Cost Per Conversion - This is how much it has cost you to achieve a conversion. You'll want to reduce your cost per conversion overtime as you optimise your AdWords campaigns and landing pages.

Cost Per Thousand (CPM) - Cost per Thousand is when you pay for impressions instead of clicks. The maximum CPM is the most you are willing to pay for one thousand impressions. This is available on the Display Network.

Daily Budget - This is the maximum you want to pay per day for advertising with Google.

Destination URL - When creating your ad you will enter a destination URL. This is the URL/page that your customer will be directed to when they click on your ad. Google is moving everyone to Final URLs which will be the new Destination URL.

Device Targeting - Google AdWords gives you the option of targeting on Desktop, Tablet and Mobile. You can choose to target Mobile or not, however, Desktop and Tablet work as one and you cannot target one but not the other.

Display Network - These are the websites, forums, blogs, etc. which aren't owned by Google but have Google ads on them. When choosing to advertise on the Display Network you are letting your ads be seen on other websites, not on the Google search results page. Make sure you set up separate Display campaigns – never mix Display and Search in the same campaign.

Display URL - This is the URL which will be seen in your ad. It does not have to be a real URL, but it does have to include your website 'home page' URL. You can add keywords after the forward slash like www.keyprinciples.co.uk/Adwords

Exact Match - This is another type of keyword. Your phrase is in square brackets and your advert only appears if someone keys into Google's search engine that exact phrase. This match type gives you maximum control as your advert will only appear if the exact phrase is used.

Impressions - The number of impressions is the number of times your ad appears on a Google search results page or other site on the Google Display Network.

Keywords - These are words or phrases which you can attach to your Ad Group which, if typed into the Google search bar, will prompt your ad to be shown on Google. Keywords are sometimes called Search Terms.

Keyword Matching Options - There are four different ways a keyword can be targeted, either Broad Match, Broad Match Modified, Phrase Match or Exact Match. There is also a Negative keywords Match.

Keyword Planner - A free Google Tool which allows you to find relevant keywords to target in your AdWords campaigns.

Landing Page - This is the website page which your customer will 'land on' when they click on your ad. You specify your landing page by inserting the appropriate URL into the Final URL field in AdWords.

Location Extension - This is the extension which allows you to show your business address below your ad so people know where you're based.

Location Targeting - This setting allows you to determine in which geographic areas your ad will appear to potential customers.

Negatives/ Negative keywords - These are terms added to your campaign or Ad Group, which you do not want to be found for. This is used so that your advert isn't shown to the wrong audience, but instead only to those who are interested in what you have to offer.

Optimisation - This is the process of ensuring that your campaign is running to its most profitable at all levels. This should include use of the Search Terms All Report, creating/editing keywords, adding negatives, adding new ads, bid adjustments, quality score checks and overall performance checks.

Organic Search Position/Organic Results - This is the non-paid for search engine ranking results.

Phrase Match - This is another type of keyword matching and is indicated by speech marks. If all the keywords that you have specified, or close variations of them, potentially with extra words included before or after the keywords you have specified, are searched for then your advert will be triggered. Since the introduction of Broad Match Modified, this match type is considered redundant by many AdWords experts.

Quality Score - This is a scoring system between 1 and 10 which Google gives you at keyword level; 1 being the worst, 10 being the best. The higher your quality scores, the better. You will pay less per click if you have a high quality score. Your score is measured by how relevant your keyword is in relation to the advert and landing page, as well as the landing page experience.

Return On Investment (ROI) - ROI is the percentage of how much profit you have made compared to how much you have spent on Google AdWords. It measures the ratio of your profits to your Google advertising costs in this instance.

Search Network - The online network which is Google and its Search Partners. Using this network will ensure your ads only appear on these sites.

Search Partners - Sites associated with Google where your Google AdWords search ads can be displayed e.g. non-Google sites such as AOL.com, AskJeeves.com, Excite.com, etc. as well as Google Maps, YouTube, etc.

Search Terms - These are the words typed into the search bar, which potentially trigger your ad to be shown.

Sitelink Extension - Another type of extension. Sitelinks are simply links which you can attach to your campaigns or Ad Groups that appear below your advert, which will take a searcher to different pages on your website. You can promote related services using sitelinks.

Social Extensions - An extension which allows you to show your social media connections and allows searchers to view your profile, and how many followers you have. For example you can link your Google+ account with your Google AdWords account.

Split Testing - The process where you run two or more adverts and/or landing pages at the same time to find the most effective.

Text Ad - An advert which is made up solely of text; these will include a headline, a display URL and two lines of text.

Topic Targeting - This is where you can target your ads to be displayed based on certain categories or topics. This is available when you set up a Google Display Network campaign.

REFERENCES

1. Perry Marshall, Mike Rhodes, Brian Todd, *Ultimate Guide to Google AdWords* (United States: Entrepreneur Press, 2014) p10.
2. Larry Kim, 'What Industries Contributed the Most to Google's Earnings?', *WordStream,* http://www.wordstream.com/articles/google-earnings [Accessed 11.03.2015].
3. Brad Geddes, *Advanced Google AdWords,* (Indiana: John Wiley & Sons, 2014) p17.
4. Brad Sugars, 'How to Calculate the Lifetime Value of a Customer', *Entrepreneur* (Aug 8, 2012) http://www.entrepreneur.com/article/224153 [Accessed 13.01.2015].
5. Larry Kim, 'What Is Quality Score & How Does it Affect PPC?', *WordStream,* http://www.wordstream.com/quality-score [Accessed 20.02.2015].
6. Richard Stokes, *Pay-Per-Click Advertising,* 2nd ed. (United States: Entrepreneur Press, 2014) p50-53.
7. Larry Kim, 'Going Unicorn Hunting: The Secrets behind Ads with 3× the Average CTR', *WordStream* (Feb 11, 2014) http://www.wordstream.com/blog/ws/2014/02/11/average-click-through-rate#good-ctr [Accessed 20.02.2015].

About The Author

Jackie Key is an entrepreneur who owns a number of successful businesses. She has over 20 years' experience in Marketing and over 10 years' experience implementing Google AdWords campaigns for clients and her own businesses too. She is a Google AdWords Advanced Search and Display Certified Consultant.

She works with businesses of all sizes from FTSE100 companies to medium size businesses, as well as small owner managed businesses and start-ups. Her international expertise extends into Europe as well as the USA.

Through creative marketing, she has helped companies grow with a primary focus on generating more leads and sales.

Jackie is a Fellow of the Chartered Institute of Marketing and has an MBA from Warwick University.

Jackie lives in West Bridgford, Nottingham, England with her partner, Emma, her daughter Lucy and the forever faithful Labrador, Rosie. Jackie loves to run, play hockey and of course walk the lovely lab, Rosie.

You can connect with Jackie via:
Facebook: www.facebook.com/JackieKeyTraining
Twitter: www.twitter.com/thejackiekey
LinkedIn: www.linkedin.com/in/jackiekey

And for the very latest tips and tricks specifically around AdWords go to **www.jackie-key.com**

Acknowledgements

This book would not have been possible without the support of Emma Fielding and Lucy Key.

Thank you to the proof readers and especially Paul Chapman for your time reading and providing feedback, and in particular to the lovely Lucy Key who read the book many times and I am sure can now set up a great AdWords campaign!

Thanks to Ellie Carr – you know how you've helped and I'm not sure I could have done it without you. Enjoy your travels.

Special thanks also to my wonderful clients. Thank you for trusting in me.

INDEX

A

Account Creation, 31-39
    About Your Business, 31
    Billing, 37
    Review, 38-39
    Your First Campaign, 32-39
Ad extensions, 59-64
    Sitelink Extension, 61-63
    Call Extensions, 62-64
    Location Extension, 63-64, 119, 121
Ad Group, 16-17, 19, 22, 23, 26, 29-30, 35-40, 42, 46, 54, 62, 67-76, 78-79, 85, 89-92
Advert, 35, 42-48, 78-79
    Ad Text, 42-45
    Advert Improvements, 42-48, 78-79

B

Benefits and Features, 43, 44, 50, 51
Bid, 35, 41, 44, 48-49, 75-79, 82, 86, 92
    Bid Optimisation, 75-79
    Bid Strategy, 33, 41
Budget, 10-11, 13, 21, 25, 33, 41, 77, 82, 84

C

Call Extensions, 47-48
Calls To Action, 36, 44, 48-50, 52
Campaign, 23-41, 71-79
    Campaign Name, 30, 41
    Campaign Optimisation, 71-79
Click Through Rate, 35, 39, 43, 48, 68, 71, 76, 78-79, 88, 90
Conversion Tracking, 54-64, 73, 77, 85
    Conversion Category, 64
    Conversion Count, 57
    Conversion Value, 56, 57
    Conversion Window, 58-59, 64

Cost Per Action (CPA), 82, 90
Cost Per Click (CPC), 70, 77, 79, 82, 91
Cost Per Impression, 82

D

Default bids, 44, 48, 54
Delivery Method, 44
Description Line, 47, 51, 57-59, 66
Devices, 41, 53-54
Display Network, 33, 105-106, 111, 113, 120-122
Display URL, 47, 54, 120
Domain, 11-12, 112

E

Exact Match, 27-28, 96, 120
Extensions, ad, 44, 59-64, 118

F

Features and Benefits, 57-58, 67-68

G

Google Analytics, 31, 64, 73, 81, 83, 113, 119
Google Display Network, 105, 120-121
      Behavioural Targeting, 107, 111
      Keyword Targeting, 107
      Managed Placement Targeting, 107-108
      Search VS Display, 106
      The Producer, 105
      Topic Targeting, 107, 122

H

Headline, 47, 51, 54-56, 64-66, 89, 96, 103, 122
History of AdWords, 3-4

I

Interruption Marketing, 108-110, 113

K

Keywords, 10, 15-29, 30-54, 56, 64, 72, 87-91, 93-104, 107, 112-113, 117, 118-122
    Broad, Phrase, Exact, 25-29
    Grouping Keywords, 24, 29, 90
    Keyword Planner, 20-24, 28, 44, 120
    Keyword Relevance, 87
    Keyword Targeting, 107

L

Landing Pages, 8, 21, 35, 47, 54, 64-71
Language, 41, 53-54
Location Extensions, 63, 118-120
Lifetime Value of Customer, 12-14, 43, 101
Location, 7, 33, 41-43, 54, 60-61, 63, 112, 118-120
    Location Extension, 63, 118-120
    Managed Placement Targeting, 107-108

N

Negative Keywords, 20, 24, 25-29, 50-51, 54, 94, 101-104, 112, 117, 120-121
Networks, 33, 41, 54, 105, 106, 111, 113, 120-121
Niche, 7-13, 112

O

Optimising Campaigns, 92-104
Organic listings, 4, 121

P

Pay Per Click (PPC), 12, 119
Peel and Stick, 89-90, 95-99, 101-104
Phrase Matches, 27-29, 120-121
Power Words, 58, 116

Q

Quality Score, 60, 67, 85-91, 95-97, 99-104, 113, 118, 121

R

Relevance, 65-66, 87-89
    Keywords, 87-89
    Ad Text, 89
    Landing Page, 65
Remarketing, 109-111

S

Sitelink Extensions, 59-61, 118, 121
Schedule Settings, 45-48
Search Network, 33, 41, 53-54, 105-107, 121
Search Terms All Report, 92-95, 101-104, 113, 121
Search VS Display, 106
Split Test, 51, 54, 64, 71, 85, 89-91, 101-104, 113, 122
Squeeze Page, 67
Structure of AdWords, 30, 53

T

Targeting, 7-10, 15-17, 20-21, 41-42, 60-61, 107-111, 119-122
    Behavioural, 107, 111
    Keyword, 107
    Location, 7, 33, 41-43, 54, 112, 120
    Managed Placement, 107-108
    Topic, 107-122
Thank you page, 74, 80-81, 84, 119
Trust signals, 68, 71

Z

Zero Impressions, 99, 102-104

Printed in Great Britain
by Amazon